rethinking sentencing

a contribution to the debate

a report from the Mission and Public Affairs Council

edited by Peter Sedgwick

CHURCH HOUSE
PUBLISHING

Church House Publishing
Church House
Great Smith Street
London SW1P 3NZ

Tel: 020 7898 1451
Fax: 020 7898 1449

ISBN 0 7151 4026 4

GS 1536

Published 2004 by Church House Publishing

Copyright © The Archbishops' Council 2004

Index copyright © Meg Davies 2004

Printed in England by The Cromwell Press, Ltd,
Trowbridge, Wiltshire

contents

contributors

David Faulkner is a Senior Research Associate at the University of Oxford Centre for Criminological Research. He was a Fellow of St John's College from 1992 until 1999, and served in the Home Office from 1959 until 1992, becoming deputy secretary in charge of the Criminal and Research and Statistics Departments in 1982. His publications include *Crime, State and Citizen* (Waterside Press, 2001), and the chapter 'Principles, Structure and a Sense of Direction' in *The Future of Criminal Justice* (SPCK, 2002).

Tim Newell was a prison governor for 30 years who ended his career as Governor of HM Prison, Grendon Underwood, which is a therapeutic establishment dealing with high-risk prisoners. He is a Quaker and gave the Swarthmore Lecture in 2000, which was published as *Forgiving Justice* (Quaker Home Service, 2000). He is active as a restorative justice facilitator in the Thames Valley area.

Stephen Pryor is a Christian who retired as a prison governor in 2002, when he published 'The Responsible Prisoner – an exploration of the extent to which imprisonment removes responsibility unnecessarily' (available on the Home Office and Prison Service web sites). Since then he has led a group exploring the connection between the prison service's and the prisoner's lack of accountability to the courts for the sentence content and delivery.

Stuart Dew works for the Churches' Criminal Justice Forum, raising awareness of criminal justice as a cause for Christian concern, and encouraging church-going people to get involved in ways that make a difference. He was, for 15 years, a probation officer, and before that a newspaper and radio journalist.

Lord Justice Laws was formerly First Junior Treasury Counsel, Common Law, and became a judge of the High Court of Justice, Queen's Bench, in 1992. Since January 1999 he has been a Lord Justice of Appeal. He is an Honorary Fellow of Robinson College, Cambridge, and Exeter College, Oxford, and has been a Judicial Visitor of University College London since 1997. He has been President of the Bar European group since 1995.

Peter Selby has been Bishop of Worcester since 1997 and Bishop to HM Prisons (in England and Wales) since 2002. He was previously William Leech Professorial Fellow in Applied Christian Theology at Durham University. The penal system has been a concern of his since his days as a theological student, and his most recent research has been in the connection between faith and economics. Both these concerns are reflected in this essay.

preface

For many people the experience of becoming caught up in the criminal justice system and then obtaining a criminal record is a traumatic one. Some may only be given a caution, but others may proceed after a trial to custody. The experience of becoming a victim of crime can also scar people for years: it is only recently that their needs have been addressed as part of a response to crime. We have in England and Wales a criminal justice system that is highly professional and which constantly seeks to execute justice amidst the complexities of our contemporary society. The Government has spent a great deal of time and effort reforming this system since it came to power in 1997, including changing the working practices of the courts, the prison and probation services as well as creating the Youth Justice Board. It remains a fact that we send far more people to prison per head of population than any other country in Western Europe, and that prison numbers are still growing while the crime rate continues to fall.

The Church is fortunate in having a report written by those who are both Christians and national experts in their field. One of the authors was Deputy Secretary at the Home Office, and is now an eminent criminologist. Two of the authors were prison governors and both are very involved in promoting restorative justice and responsible sentencing. Both of these topics are explained lucidly in their contributions. There are also articles by the Criminal Justice Officer of the Churches' Criminal Justice Forum, a judge from the Court of Appeal and the Bishop to Prisons. Such contributions mean that the report is both comprehensive and challenging.

These essays are commissioned by the Mission and Public Affairs Council. The Council welcomes the publication of this collection as a contribution to encourage debate. Such a debate will echo the fact that a vigorous argument on why, and how, people should be punished has been at the centre of national life for the last decade. This report attempts to look behind the sound bites of politicians and the tabloids and to bring to bear on this subject an informed and Christian contribution. I hope that this report will be widely read both inside and outside the churches.

✠ Tom Butler
Bishop of Southwark
Vice-chair, Public Affairs, Mission and Public Affairs Council

introduction

Peter Sedgwick

This is the first time since 1991 that General Synod has discussed a report on sentencing and the role of the courts. In 1991 the Board for Social Responsibility published *Crime, Justice and the Demands of the Gospel*,[1] and this report was debated in Synod. In 1999 a further report called *Prisons: a Study in Vulnerability*[2] was also debated, with the emphasis on those who were most vulnerable in prison, such as the young people, the mentally ill, women and sex offenders. In addition, the report looked at the vulnerability of prisoners' families, and how chaplaincy could respond to these needs. Synod was addressed on that occasion before the debate by Martin Narey, who was then Director General of Prisons.

Much has changed since 1999. In particular, the Government has carried out a wide-ranging review of sentencing policy, much of which was enshrined in the Criminal Justice and Sentencing Act, together with the Courts Act and the Anti-Social Behaviour Act. At the same time, restorative justice has become increasingly important as an alternative to traditional ways of sentencing, especially, but not only, in youth justice. There is also now a CTBI network coordinating the Churches' work in criminal justice, called the Churches' Criminal Justice Forum, which employs three staff, working on policy, education and resettlement of offenders.

For all these reasons it is appropriate that another report should be commissioned by the Church of England's Mission and Public Affairs Council. *Rethinking Sentencing* shows how the debate on the future of sentencing will affect all our lives, from the referral panel helping young offenders make reparation to their victims to the issues of social inclusion, civic renewal and zero tolerance for antisocial behaviour. There is one chapter on prisons, but its emphasis is on how life in prison contributes to a loss of responsibility among prisoners. The report shows how churches are involved with issues of criminal justice across the country, and how such topics as punishment, reparation and healing raise profound theological questions. How we pass sentence on another through the agency of the courts and the bodies that express restorative justice is inevitably a deeply searching issue for Christians.

The final conversation Jesus had before he died on the cross involved a criminal saying to him 'In our case it is plain justice: we are paying the price for our misdeeds. But this man has done nothing wrong' (Luke 23.41)[3]. This report asks 'what is "plain justice"?' and whether the only response to crime is to pay the price for misdeeds. In John's Gospel Jesus places the authority of Pilate to pass sentence on him under the authority of God (John 19.11). By what authority do we punish one another, and what place does restoration have in all this? These are the issues raised by this report and which should concern all Christians.

Peter Sedgwick

Chair, Churches' Criminal Justice Forum

chapter 1

the reform of sentencing and the future of the criminal courts

David Faulkner

> Do not judge, and you will not be judged; do not condemn, and you will not be condemned. Forgive, and you will be forgiven; give, and it will be given to you. A good measure, pressed down, shaken together, running over, will be put into your lap; for the measure you give will be the measure you get back (Luke 6.37-8).

Those words are a warning against a purely retributive, utilitarian or instrumental view of sentencing, and an inspiration to those who are trying to promote a more reparative understanding of justice.

The first account in Western literature of a criminal trial is probably the description of the shield that the god Hephaestus made for the hero Achilles in Homer's *Iliad*. The shield shows a scene in which a trial is taking place over the penalty to be paid for a man's death. The defendant has offered to pay restitution; the victim's family refuses to accept it. The family's acceptance will bring an end to the matter – what might today be called 'closure'. Refusal will lead to a blood feud between the two families that might continue from generation to generation. The issue is referred to a judge or arbitrator, who calls in the elders of the community to form what might now be called a sentencing circle. The scene shows an early recognition that, in a settled society, the effects of a crime cannot be satisfactorily resolved by the parties on their own, others have a stake in the outcome, and a wider public interest is involved. Classical scholars have interpreted the text in different ways, but the issue the elders are being called on to decide is in effect a choice between retributive and reparative justice.[1]

Later societies and cultures, in Roman, Anglo-Saxon, medieval and Tudor times, resolved the issue in different ways. Over time, retribution became more prominent, victims' interests became less significant, and the state – in England, the Crown – came increasingly to take charge of the process.

the liberal tradition

The Enlightenment brought other influences – to promote a scientific basis for knowledge, to challenge traditional morality, and to question, control and regulate the power of the state. It created the liberal tradition in Western criminal justice.[2] Radzinowicz described its features as including a belief in free will; criminal responsibility; punishment proportionate to the seriousness of the offence; retribution and deterrence as the major, if not exclusive, functions of punishment; strict definition of criminal offences; no retroactivity; judicial independence; openness and accountability; respect for the rule of law; and the presumption of innocence.[3] Others might add the minimum use of imprisonment and respect for human dignity, equality and human rights.

From a broader social perspective, the liberal tradition can be seen as assuming a foundation of principles, especially the principle that people are of equal value and deserve equal respect as human beings, regardless of race, nationality, gender, religion or disability. At its best, it applies this principle regardless of differences in people's authority or status, and it demands a sense of 'common belonging' so that members of minority or disadvantaged groups (for example) can feel at home in their wider society,[4] and the majority recognize them as members of that society and show them the same consideration and respect. The state should not intervene unnecessarily in the lives of its citizens; when it does so, the intervention should be proportionate to a legitimate need or purpose; citizens should have accessible procedures for appeal or redress if they believe they have been unjustly treated; and they should have some voice, or at least an opportunity for a voice, on decisions that affect them directly as individuals or which concern the well-being of their society or communities.[5]

The liberal tradition is now coming under criticism, from different directions. From one point of view, it reflects the notion of the 'nation state', whose time, the American writer Philip Bobbitt argues, came to a close with the ending of the Cold War, to be replaced by the 'market state', based on maximizing opportunities and satisfying expectations and demands.[6] From another, it is seen as too tolerant and complacent, as allowing too pluralist an understanding of citizenship and national identity, and as failing to insist on the unified culture, values and discipline that are thought to be needed to meet the modern threats to morality and social cohesion. Those threats may come from permissiveness and 'political correctness', from international terrorism, or even, as some people have claimed, from Islam.[7] From a third and opposite point of view, it fails to provide adequate recognition or protection for ethnic and cultural minorities. From a fourth, it could be criticized as expecting too much from citizens and civil society, and as diminishing the role of the state to a point where its effectiveness could be undermined and its legitimacy called into question. From a less intellectual position, several writers and commentators, and even some ministers, have expressed dissatisfaction with systems of law or legal process that are designed to formalize and protect human rights.[8]

Neither the liberal tradition, nor the criminal justice process as it now operates, allow much space for compassion, mercy, reconciliation or forgiveness. Appeals to those values can be found in Shakespeare, for example in Portia's appeal to the quality of mercy in *The Merchant of Venice*, and in Isabella's appeal for pity in *Measure for Measure*,[9] but there is not much authority for them in legislation or jurisprudence. The great jurists of the eighteenth century, for example Blackstone, Mansfield and Romilly, had a lot to say about freedom, but very little about compassion.

From a Christian perspective, Tim Gorringe has written of the need to shift the balance from individual satisfaction to biblical conceptions of redemption and reconciliation.[10] David McIlroy has argued that the law has to be interpreted through the Holy Spirit,[11] and Christopher Marshall and Stuart Dew that, for the Christian, prisons and prisoners can never be left 'out of sight, out of mind' and criminal justice must always be matter of acute concern.[12] Jonathan Burnside has written of the biblical belief that true justice is inspired by God and of the biblical implications for the modern process of justice. They include the integrity of the system for appointing judges, and the danger of imposing too many restrictions on judges' discretion. They are especially relevant to the Government's proposals for an independent judicial appointments board, and, although bribery is not an issue for today's judges, there may be comparable questions about the attention that they should pay to the pressure of popular opinion or campaigns by newspapers.[13] In more recent work, he has considered the Bible's support for proportionality in punishment, although not as an absolute principle; the fact that biblical law frequently assumes a background of negotiation between the parties, with obligations on both sides; and the need for communities as well as individuals, agencies and institutions to be involved. Crime control and criminal justice have to be reconnected with broader themes of social justice and social reconstruction; and punishment should reach beyond the individual offender and victim and the executive agencies to effect some repair to the social fabric. Not everything can be put right through the criminal justice process, and outstanding injustice must be left ultimately with God.[14]

the politicization of criminal justice

Criminal justice has always been a political issue but it did not feature prominently in party politics until the late 1970s, when the experience of crime was becoming more widespread among the electorate and especially among the middle class.[15] From then until the mid-1990s the Conservative Party believed it had a political advantage in depicting their opponents as 'soft on crime', partly because the Labour Party in opposition had traditionally been inclined to associate crime with poverty and economic disadvantage, rather than weakness in law enforcement or lack of severity in sentencing.[16] From the mid-1990s onwards, the Labour Party responded vigorously with its slogan 'Tough on crime, tough on the causes of crime' and both main parties have since then competed to demonstrate which can be more 'tough' – in effect, which party can cause offenders to be punished more severely. Very little has separated the main parties in practice, and such opposition as there has been to governments of either of the main parties has come mainly from 'liberal' newspapers, and individuals in the House of Lords. Bishops have taken an active, non-political part in debates in the House of Lords, including especially Robert Hardy when he was Bishop of Lincoln and Bishop for prisons. The Board for Social Responsibility's report *Crime, Justice and the Demands of the Gospel*[17] made an important, and politically impartial, contribution to the debate at the time of the Criminal Justice Act 1991.

The politicization of criminal justice has another significant aspect in the much closer attention that ministers and their political advisers now pay to the detailed formulation of policy, to law enforcement and the administration of justice, and to the presentation of their policies to the public. That development could be observed from the mid-1960s onwards, but it accelerated after the change of government in 1979 and did so dramatically after the change in 1997. One indication is the increase in the volume and complexity of criminal justice legislation (the Labour Government introduced 17 criminal justice Bills between 1997 and 2003), another is the frequency of administrative reorganization, and a third is the increasing range and detail of the politically imposed targets and performance indicators to which services are required to conform.[18] Decisions that were once a matter of professional or administrative judgement are increasingly taken politically by ministers, or by officials in what has become a political context. The White Paper *Justice for All*[19] is an aggressively political document, quite different in style and presentation from those published on similar subjects during the 1980s.

responses to crime

Most governments, and most people, have in modern times come to see the country's response to crime as essentially a matter for the state, and in particular for the criminal justice system. That response then becomes a matter of detection, trial and punishment, to which the individual citizen should make a contribution by cooperating with the police, giving evidence in court, and sometimes by serving as a juror or lay magistrate, but in which he or she otherwise has no role or responsibility. Governments for their part have come to see their task not just as one of administering and regulating the process through legislation and financial control, as they did for the most part until the 1980s, but as one that also demands ministers' direct intervention or detailed oversight.

As crime increased and criminal justice became more politicized, ministers became increasingly frustrated by their apparent inability to reduce crime or to improve the public's confidence in the process. Declining rates of conviction, and the discovery that only about two per cent of crime is brought to a conviction in court,[20] were a particular source of irritation. Ministers' reaction has not, on the whole, been to look for new ways of reducing crime or of repairing the damage, but to try to make criminal justice itself 'more effective'.[21] As well as seeking to improve efficiency by reducing delays and increasing detections and convictions, their policies have widened the scope of the criminal law, extended the reach of the criminal justice process, and tightened its grip.[22] Successive governments have introduced legislation to create new criminal offences at a rate of between 100 and 150 offences a year. The results have included an increase in the severity of sentencing and a rise in the prison population of over 75 per cent over 12 years (from 42,000 in 1991 to 75,400 in March 2004). Many more people, including children, are either in prison or under some form of supervision and control, and that control may be of a more intrusive or intensive kind, by, for example, electronic monitoring. Almost the whole population is regularly observed by television cameras. Statistics show that crime is falling, but many people refuse to believe the figures. It is difficult to attribute the fall to any particular policy or initiative, or to judge the effect of other factors such as the state of the economy or exclusions from school.

The present Government, more than any other in recent times, has seemed determined that 'protecting the public', both from crime itself and from the loss, injury or fear caused by crime and social nuisance, is a responsibility it has to take upon itself. It has also been more ambitious in its claims that crime can be significantly reduced by changes in law enforcement, sentencing and penal practice. David Blunkett has said that 'social order is the first responsibility of government' and that he regards the expansion of criminal justice to deal with problems of social disorder as part of a policy of social renewal.[23] That view can be connected to a more general attitude on the part of government, which places great emphasis on the management and, so far as possible, the elimination or avoidance of risk – whether it is a risk to the public (for example from crime, accidents or disease), an operational failure (perhaps of a computer system), or a threat to the Government's own political standing and reputation.[24] Drawing on Philip Bobbitt's work already mentioned, Archbishop Rowan Williams has characterized that attitude as treating government as a matter of 'insurance' against the hazards of what is seen as an increasingly insecure global and political environment, and of the shift to a new political mode associated with the 'market state'.[25] Ministers, for their part, seem to see the change more as a transition to a more democratic, responsive and accountable style of government in which they can take some pride.

Four characteristics distinguish the present Government's approach to criminal justice from that of its predecessor. The first is its much more active approach to youth justice and its attempt, through the Youth Justice Board, to make more children the subject of criminal justice interventions and to do so at an earlier stage in their lives. The second is its emphasis on rehabilitation and reform (or perhaps, more accurately, the prevention of reoffending) through various compulsory forms of intervention and supervision. The third is its insistence on rigorous enforcement of court orders, conditions and requirements, with severe penalties for those who do not comply. The fourth is its determination to tackle antisocial behaviour by extending criminal sanctions to forms of behaviour that are not necessarily criminal or particularly serious in themselves, but which can be a serious nuisance if they are persistent or widespread, or which may show irresponsibility on the part of parents or others with a duty of care.[26] Those policies are based partly on the belief that they will reduce crime – as they may do to some extent but, because so many other factors will always be involved, it will be hard to say to what extent or at what cost – but they also seem to be founded on moral conviction. The Government's attitude led first to the Auld and Halliday reviews of the courts and of the sentencing framework, then to the White Papers *Justice for All* and *Respect and Responsibility*,[27] and finally to the large volume of criminal justice legislation that Parliament enacted in 2003.

the function of sentencing

When the state punishes a convicted offender it can be seen as performing any or all of three separate functions. The first is declaratory and retributive – to uphold the law, to condemn, to punish. The test is 'has justice been done?' The second is utilitarian and instrumental – to protect the public and reduce crime. That can be achieved in various ways – physical control of the offender (typically by imprisonment, but also increasingly by electronic means), deterrence, or rehabilitation. The test is whether the method used 'works' or is 'effective'.[28] The third is reparative – to repair the damage, to achieve some form of reconciliation, to compensate the victim. Here the test is harder to establish. It may be a feeling of satisfaction or relief on the part of those who have been affected by the offence, or a sense among some or all of them that it is now possible to 'move on'. But it is more than simply an absence of reoffending, the personal satisfaction of an individual victim, or public applause.

Each of the three functions has come into prominence at different times. Retribution – or 'just deserts' – was prominent in the 1980s and in the Criminal Justice Act 1991; the instrumental view was prominent in the 1960s and again in the 1990s, especially after the change of government in 1997, and it is reflected in the Criminal Justice Act 2003. The reparative view has never been as pervasive as the other two and it has not been so clearly articulated, but it is now gaining ground. It has emerged partly as a response to the system's long-standing neglect of victims, but also to correct what is sometimes seen as the system's remoteness from 'real life' and ordinary experience. Anthony Duff, for example, has considered a more 'communicative' process of sentencing in which victims and communities would be more directly involved and which would look not for conventional punishment but for reparation and repair (although it would still include punishment of a different kind). He hopes in that way to achieve a resolution of what others have seen as a fundamental conflict between the different views of sentencing and punishment.[29] The best-known and most obvious expression of the reparative function of sentencing is, of course, restorative justice, which is the subject of the next chapter.

Each of the three functions of sentencing implies a different set of purposes, considerations and criteria – for example, the weight to be given to proportionality, previous record, social background or mitigating circumstances – and it is confusing to judge a sentence that is intended to serve one function by criteria that are more appropriate to another. It is possible, and it has historically been the practice, to see the court as concerned with the retributive function – to decide the amount of punishment that is needed to match the seriousness of the offence and the culpability of the offender; and the executive, principally the prison and probation services, as responsible for the instrumental function. That distinction is consistent with the traditional 'liberal' view that the punishment consists in the sentence of the court, not in the offender's treatment after sentence has been passed. The sentencer's responsibility is to apply the law in accordance with precedent and statute, not to consider longer-term outcomes, wider social consequences, cost, or the services' capacity to give effect to the sentences imposed. The services have to do the best they can with the offenders who are placed in their charge, the resources that are available, and the targets and performance indicators that are set by government, but they are not concerned with those wider social factors that may also affect the outcome. No authority or agency has claimed any special ownership or responsibility for the reparative function, and sceptics might question whether it can be accommodated at all in an adversarial system of justice. As Stephen Pryor points out in Chapter 3, offenders themselves have no responsibilities except to comply with their sentences and the demands that are made on them.

That simple, or it might be said, simplistic, division – and denial – of responsibility makes quite good practical sense of what is inevitably a complex situation. It was more or less implicit in the Criminal Justice Act 1991. But it is no longer acceptable, if it ever was, to make such a firm distinction between the retributive and instrumental function of sentencing, or between the role of the courts and of what is now to be called the National Offender Management Service. It becomes impossible when the reparative function also has to be taken into account. Confusion inevitably arises when the three functions have to be divided between two constitutionally separate types of organization, and then reconciled and combined in a single sentencing decision.

sentencing reform

The Criminal Justice Act, the Courts Act and the Anti-Social Behaviour Act, all passed in 2003, are together intended to bring about a major reform of the criminal justice process and of the system that operates it. They are, in the words of the White Paper *Justice for All*,[30] guided by a 'single clear priority', which is 'to rebalance the criminal justice system in favour of the victim and the community so as to reduce crime and bring more offenders to justice'. They are to 'put the sense back into sentencing'.

Several of the provisions in the Criminal Justice Act attracted criticism when the Bill was before Parliament. They included those that allow previous convictions to be used as evidence of guilt; the retrial of certain serious offences after a previous verdict of 'not guilty'; restrictions on access to trial before a jury; and minimum or presumptive terms of imprisonment for offences of murder or which involve firearms. Parliament gave less attention to the provisions on sentencing, although they are likely to have a greater effect in the longer term.

The Act sets out five statutory purposes of sentencing: the punishment of offenders; the reduction of crime, including the effect of deterrence; the reform and rehabilitation of offenders; the protection of the public; and the making of reparation. Those purposes correspond more or less with the functions of sentencing that were discussed earlier in this chapter, but there is no recognition of the differences between them or of the implications of those differences. The Act provides that sentences are to be proportionate to the seriousness of the offence, but previous convictions are to be treated as an aggravating factor. There is to be a new, single form of community sentence, which can contain any of twelve possible conditions or requirements. There is to be a new range of sentences that will in different ways combine elements of custody and of supervision in the community, and a new set of life or extended sentences of imprisonment for offenders who are considered to be dangerous.

These are complicated provisions, and different and sometimes conflicting considerations will arise in individual cases. Sentencing is to be consistent, but it is not clear how consistency is to relate to the nature of the offence, the situation and culpability of the offender, or the intended purpose of the sentence among those that are now set out in statute. All those considerations are overridden for certain serious offences that are to attract a minimum or presumptive sentence. When considering a sentence, the court is presumably intended to decide, and to state, which of the statutory purposes the particular sentence is to serve.

But the means of achieving those purposes are in the hands of executive agencies – mainly in future the National Offender Management Service – and outside the control of the court. They also depend on the offender's acceptance by his or her community and by society as a whole. That division of responsibility, and the lack of coherence and accountability that could result from it, may become a source of frustration if the statutory purposes are to be taken seriously. Research has shown the confusion that has already been generated by the combination of complicated legislation, mixed messages and external pressures.[31] Stephen Pryor develops the argument in Chapter 3 of this volume.

The mechanism intended to resolve those problems is the Sentencing Guidelines Council. Supported by the existing Sentencing Advisory Panel, it is to establish a new and comprehensive framework of guidelines for particular offences, and also to issue guidance that will resolve the possible sources of confusion. If it is successful, the creation of the Council may come to be seen as the Act's most significant achievement. But the Council has a huge and complex task, involving extensive consultation and political sensitivity in its relations with government, Parliament and the judiciary. The Council and the Panel will need access to, or their own capacity for, rigorous research and analysis so that they can estimate and then assess the effects of their guidance on the numbers and types of sentence imposed. They will need to consider the resulting demands on resources, and especially on the services' capacity to give effect to those sentences, and any differential and potentially unjust impact there might be, for example on children, women or ethnic minorities.

The passage of the Act was closely followed by the report *Managing Offenders, Reducing Crime,*[32] and the Government's accompanying statement *Reducing Crime – Changing Lives.*[33] The report has two features that distinguish it from any other government-sponsored report in recent times. One is its clear statement of the need for a closer alignment between sentencing practice and the capacity of the system to give effect to the sentences imposed, with a reduction in the size of the prison population and of the number of offenders under supervision in the community from those that are at present projected, and with fines replacing community sentences for many less serious offences and low-risk offenders. The other is the separation of 'offender management', including the commissioning of accommodation and programmes, from the actual provision of those facilities. They would be commissioned in accordance with a principle of 'contestability', which would admit a wider range of providers, including providers from the private and voluntary and community sectors. Commissioning would be devolved to the nine English regions and to Wales. The aim, and the assumption, is that the changes in sentencing and the new administrative structure will together enable sentences to be 'targeted' more accurately, and resources to be used more 'effectively', so that the outcome will be a reduction in reoffending and, therefore, in the overall level of crime. The Government's statement describes the report as a 'once in a generation opportunity'.

Reactions to the report were still being formed at the time when this chapter was being written. Those expressed so far ranged from an enthusiastic welcome to deep scepticism – a welcome for the fact that the problem of matching demand to capacity had at last been recognized and a radical solution proposed; scepticism because of a fear that the proposed solution might be unrealistically ambitious (politically and practically), or that it might be arbitrarily imposed without consultation.

This is an uncertain and precarious situation. Time and effort are needed to translate the intentions and the detailed provisions of the Act into fair, consistent and intelligible sentencing practice. The fact that the Act and the report are being implemented during a period of exceptionally severe pressure on resources will inevitably affect the timing and coherence of the process. The combination of legislative change, administrative upheaval and operational pressure will demand a high standard of political and professional leadership and the most skilled and careful management. The Act is unlikely to be the last word in sentencing reform, even for the next few years, and the report provides only an outline, with the details still to be decided. Both will require a continuous process of reconsideration, revision and adjustment as anomalies, injustices, inefficiencies and perhaps emergencies arise and have to be resolved.

children and young people

Britain is deeply ambivalent in its attitude towards children and young people. On the one hand, children are seen as a blessing, to be loved and cherished and to be nurtured as the foundation for the nation's future. Their rights have to be protected and respected; in many situations their welfare should take precedence over other considerations. On the other, children are unruly, noisy, inconsiderate, and an unwelcome nuisance as neighbours or in public places. They have to be kept in order. They have to be protected from danger and kept out of trouble, but once they are in trouble they should know the difference between right and wrong and they or their parents should be punished accordingly.

Government policy towards children has four main, and very distinct, strands: universal (in theory) education directed towards skills and qualifications; social and economic measures to reduce the extent to which children grow up in poverty; child protection for those at risk of neglect or abuse; and youth justice for those who break the law or – increasingly – whose behaviour is antisocial but not necessarily criminal. All four strands are receiving a great deal of attention, but each is being pursued independently. And yet the children who are the focus of those policies – those who do not make progress or who are excluded or truant from school, who live in poverty, who suffer neglect or abuse, or who become involved in offending – are very often the same or come from the same families and backgrounds.

Archbishop Rowan Williams has said that 'for all our corporate sentimentality about childhood, and for all our well-meant protocols about the protection of children, thousands of our children in Britain are invisible and their sufferings unnoticed'.[34] He argues that the challenge is to become a country that takes children seriously by thinking ahead and not simply reacting to crises, with questions to be answered about the responsibilities of families, schools, the youth justice system and national government. Reforms of youth justice have brought better coordination and understanding between the services, especially through the formation of youth offending teams. Legislation has made a range of new and potentially valuable orders and programmes – reparation orders, action plan orders, referral orders, drug treatment and testing orders, parenting orders – available to the youth courts, with corresponding programmes of treatment and activity. Intensive surveillance and supervision programmes can be provided for persistent offenders as an alternative to custody. There is some evidence of success in reducing reoffending, which legislation has made the single aim and effectively the most important test. Most of the success has so far been associated with the less severe forms of sentence or disposal, but it is too soon to make any final judgement. The changes proposed in the Green Paper *Every Child Matters*[35] should improve the arrangements for protecting children at risk. A companion document *Youth Justice – the Next Steps*[36] proposes further reforms of youth justice, principally to simplify the structure of sentencing and strengthen the provision for juvenile offenders that is available in the community.

The Audit Commission's report *Youth Justice 2004*[37] and the National Audit Office's report *Youth Offending: The Delivery of Community and Custodial Sentences*[38] have reviewed the progress that has been made since the Audit Commission's earlier report in 1996. They concluded that the Government's reforms have generally been successful and that the situation has significantly improved over that period, but more needs to be done to improve communications and administration and to achieve a stronger recognition that 'mainstream agencies, such as schools and health services, should take full responsibility for preventing offending by young people'.[39]

Even so, there remains an artificial, and for the child often accidental, division between civil and social measures on the one hand and criminal proceedings on the other. There is an increasing temptation, which the Government has encouraged, for the authorities to look to criminal proceedings and criminal sanctions as being 'more effective' despite their criminalizing and 'net-widening' consequences. The new arrangements are being operated on the ground with some optimism and enthusiasm,[40] but they have been severely criticized by some academics for their emphasis on criminalization and punishment. It is a sad commentary on British society that it should be so difficult to restore someone's childhood; that in 2004 almost 3,000 children should be in prison institutions compared with half that number ten years before; that conditions in those institutions should still fall so far below a satisfactory standard; and that, despite the criticisms of HM Chief Inspector of Prisons and all the children's and penal reform organizations, the situation should attract so little public anger or even concern.[41] The old approved schools, abolished by the Children Act 1969, had many faults, but at least they were schools and not prisons.

For children and young people, the best way forward for sentencing and the courts may not be to go on extending the role and scope for criminal justice, but to focus on educational and social measures and institutions, to reduce the use of custody, and to develop alternative forms of provision and of residential accommodation where it is needed. In the longer term, although this is not politically realistic at present, the age of criminal responsibility ought to be raised progressively from 10 to 14 and eventually 16, as it is in most other European countries; and ministerial responsibility for both civil and criminal matters affecting children ought to be brought together in a single government department, separate from the Home Office.

social inclusion and active citizenship – the longer term

The White Paper *Justice for All*,[42] and the subsequent legislation, are an expression of the Government's policies for the state to reduce crime and exercise social control by expanding the criminal law and reinforcing the criminal justice process. There is, however, another, less prominent but equally significant, strand in government policy. The Home Office Strategic Framework states that:

> Our purpose is to build a safe, just and tolerant society, so our role is to promote both:
>
> Social inclusion and active citizenship
>
> Effective enforcement of law, order and our borders.

The paper suggests that both aspects should be of equal importance.[43]

During the summer of 2003, the Home Secretary, David Blunkett, published a paper on 'civil renewal', which, he believes, 'must form the centrepiece of the government's reform agenda for the coming years'.[44] His paper starts with a number of reflections on the nature of citizenship and democracy; on freedom, duty and obligation, including the nature and role of the state; and on community and social control. It continues with some comments on existing policies, including the reform of public services; and then sets out proposals for new reforms in the police and in criminal justice more generally, and for the creation of 'community courts' and a new Centre for Active Citizenship. In a separate paper, Hazel Blears has called for new forms of ownership and involvement by citizens or communities in public services, especially those in the areas of health and education.[45] Meanwhile, the Cabinet Office and the Office for National Statistics developed the idea of 'social capital', which they define as 'networks together with shared norms, values and understandings that facilitate co-operation within or among groups'; its main aspects are 'citizenship, neighbourliness, trust and shared values, community involvement, volunteering, social networks, and civil political participation'.[46]

Several of the Government's existing policies can be seen as promoting social inclusion and active citizenship. They include, for example, Sure Start, the New Deal for Communities, the Connexions Service, and the work of the Social Exclusion Unit in the Cabinet Office and of the Communities Group, including the Active Communities Directorate and the Social Renewal Unit in the Home Office, together with the Government's commitment to racial equality as expressed in the Race Relations (Amendment) Act 2000. They can also be seen in the Government's encouragement for citizens to become more actively involved in the criminal justice process as magistrates, through service on juries, or as members of referral panels for juveniles. A significant difference in what is now being proposed is that, after several years of central direction and control, the Government seems ready to contemplate and even to encourage a movement towards local responsibility, discretion and empowerment.

Ideas such as 'social inclusion' and 'active citizenship', and the related ideas of community and social responsibility, can be interpreted in different ways. They can be interpreted openly, in the spirit of the liberal tradition described earlier in this chapter; or restrictively, as a way of demanding social conformity and of insisting on compliance with norms and expectations as a condition of social acceptance. Failure to comply then brings punishment, and leads to social exclusion and a denial of access to legitimate social capital. The contrast has been more fully discussed elsewhere.[47] The balance that a government, a society, a community or a religion finds between the two sets of attitudes and approaches will change over time, but the balance is one of the features that defines its character. It is difficult at this stage to tell how far the Government is prepared to go in promoting local responsibility and discretion, how far local communities and the general public are willing or able to accept it, or if the outcome will be a society that becomes more 'safe, just and tolerant', more generous, confident and compassionate, or one that is more fearful, populist and punitive.

citizenship and the courts

The relationship between citizenship and the courts is a complex matter. It is certainly part of the duties and responsibilities of citizenship to appear as a witness, to cooperate with the court and tell the truth, and to serve as a juror if called upon to do so. Appointment as a magistrate is an obvious and important example of a citizen's service to the public. Successive governments have claimed to support 'local justice', at least at the level of the magistrates' courts, although the thrust of government policy has for 20 years been towards greater standardization and uniformity, with the closure of smaller courts in the interests of efficiency and a strong emphasis on consistency of practice. (It could be said that in this respect they have followed a tradition that goes back to Henry II.)

The whole point of the adversarial system of justice, as it operates in Great Britain and other common law countries, has been to detach the criminal trial from the complex set of relationships and responsibilities that make up the ideas of citizenship as they are discussed in this paper. The criminal trial is a contest to decide on the defendant's guilt – not on his or her innocence – according to the law, and then to impose a sentence that conforms to the expectations described earlier in this chapter. Ideas of citizenship have been relevant where they are concerned with respect for the defendant's dignity and humanity, with the fairness of the trial, with the proportionality of the sentence and with an offender's rights of appeal. The courts have not been concerned with the rights or responsibilities, still less the interests or feelings, of others who may be involved in the situation. Considerations of that kind may sometimes be brought into the process – the impact of the offence on the victim and the victim's feelings about it, or the offender's relationship with and responsibility for his or her family – but as matters of aggravation or mitigation that are marginal to the proceedings as a whole.

Magistrates and juries (though not judges) can be thought of as representing their local communities, although that is harder in urban than in rural areas, and they are not in any significant sense accountable to those communities. Ministers have said that they would like victims to be more closely involved in the criminal justice system, but so far – and most people would probably say rightly – on limited terms that do not extend to any sense of 'ownership' of, or access to, the court's decision-making process. The Government has announced its intention to reform the method by which judges are appointed in order to give it more legitimacy and to widen the social and cultural background from which appointments are made. But there has been no suggestion, and no serious demand, that citizens should be more actively involved, for example by instituting a system by which judges would be elected or made more directly accountable to the public.

There has been a similar attitude towards sentencing. On one view, which has probably been that of most judges and magistrates, sentencing is – like the rest of the criminal trial – a function that is undertaken on behalf of the state. It is a matter between the judge or magistrates and the individual offender, in which other citizens are not involved and have no standing. That view can reasonably be sustained for the process of establishing guilt in a contested trial (but with the significant addition of a jury in trials at the Crown Court), but the process of sentencing is clearly different from that of establishing guilt. Different considerations and different kinds of judgement are involved, and there is no obvious reason (apart from convenience) why the same adjudicating authority or the same forum should be equally suitable for both. There has already been a move towards a separation of roles in the formation of referral panels in youth justice.

In his paper on civil renewal, David Blunkett[48] has proposed the development of 'community court', drawing on examples in the United States. A pilot project is being set up in Liverpool. Experience has shown that models in criminal justice are not easily transferred between one jurisdiction and another,[49] and his particular model of the Red Hook Community Justice Center in New York may be difficult to accommodate within the existing or proposed frameworks for court administration and sentencing in England and Wales.[50] But a programme that enabled the police, the prison and probation services, the Crown Prosecution Service and, importantly, defence lawyers to establish a stronger sense of local identity and responsibility, and to work more constructively with other agencies and with civil society in a spirit of social inclusion and active citizenship, provides an opportunity for serious and potentially fundamental reform. If the reforms proposed in the Carter Report are pursued in the same spirit, the outcome could transform both the process of criminal justice and the culture of the statutory services, the courts and the practising legal profession. Later chapters discuss some of the possibilities in more detail.

conclusions

The process of change and incremental reform will clearly continue, whether it is driven by a long-term vision of the nature of justice in a modern society, by political expediency and opportunism, or simply by events. Critical factors are likely to be the progress that can be made in establishing the reparative function of sentencing as part of the 'normal' criminal justice process, and the extent to which responsibility for preventing and responding to crime, including sentencing, can be recognized and shared more widely in society as a whole. The outcomes from that process will depend not only on the nature of the reforms themselves, but also, and perhaps even more importantly, on the spirit in which they are put into effect and on the nature of British society more generally. That spirit may be one of tolerance, compassion, humanity and trust. Or it may be one of rejection, vindictiveness, self-gratification and fear. Christians, and all people of good will, can affect how that choice is made.

chapter 2

restorative justice in England

Tim Newell

introduction

Restorative justice is a historical response to the crisis of purpose, identity and conscience that is facing the criminal justice system. While the current criminal justice system sees crime as the breaking of the law, and violation of the 'King's Peace', restorative justice sees crime as a violation of human relationships. Thus, where the current system aims at protecting the public and inculcating civil responsibility by insisting on a philosophy of retribution and punishment, restorative justice aims at promoting accountability by healing the harm. Justice, in the current system, has little scope for serving as a means of reconciliation and reconnection to the community. Indeed, even as far as its stated aim of rehabilitation is concerned, the current system has been found seriously wanting. Restorative justice, by contrast, draws on a variety of healing and transforming processes to effect public safety by transforming the damaged relationships through an experience of heightened awareness of the damage and a commitment to active responsibility in response. Without addressing the crisis of purpose, the problems that lead to a lack of confidence in the system, such as low clear up rates, delays in the process and prison overcrowding, are unlikely to be solved.

The term restorative justice was used by Albert Eglash[1] when he claimed that there are three types of criminal justice:

1. retributive justice based on punishment

2. distributive justice based on therapeutic treatment of offenders

3. restorative justice based on restitution.

Christian theology stresses salvation by grace and not by the law, in validating the truth of the gospel. However, in relation to the criminal justice system, we rely on the law. In 'A Christian Approach to Criminal

Justice' Marlin states that 'in spite of the Reformation recovery of the gospel, not a single Protestant society, alas, applied the principle of justification by faith to the criminal justice process ... Rather all Protestant societies have persistently continued to impose fines (indulgences) and prisons (purgatory) as the way to expiate offences (and to pay one's debt to society).'[2] Punishing the offender could be seen as the antithesis of the gospel vision, for, as Marlin says about punishment, 'You can be restored to society, justified, only by expiating your offence under law'. He searches for justice that reflects the gospel instead of the tradition of Roman law, feudal custom, Anglo-Saxon precedent and other non-Christian influences.

Of more practical significance for us in considering theological influences is the application of the concept of scapegoating, about which René Girard has written.[3] Christianity's marriage with the legal system of the Roman Empire, added to the dynamics of scapegoating, has ensured that we have developed the dysfunctional system that causes so much concern at present.[4]

The concept of the original penitentiary was a humane response to the brutalization of criminal justice. Its purpose was as a means of penitence to help offenders turn around their life through a process of quiet contemplation on the harms done. This system went very astray, with architecture and the physical and psychological isolation of prisoners leading to a new brutalization that prevented the very rehabilitation for which the original penitentiaries had been ostensibly designed.

The biggest obstacle for the implementation of a humanitarian approach, which restores losses to victims and facilitates peace and tranquillity among opposing parties, is our addiction to vengeance, the underlying force behind many current criminal justice policies. The pain and fear caused by crime results in ever greater demands for the punishment of offenders, as if there is no other way to stop the violence. Our addiction to punishment is reflected in our call for more prisons, longer sentences and more police officers, and demonstrates the state's need, and our addiction, for social control. But beneath that lies a more powerful obstacle yet. The self-delusion that offenders are wholly bad, wholly determined to destroy the social fabric and wholly insensitive to suffering, allows us to use punishments that exclude, incapacitate and permit vengeance, however much we dress that up by using words like 'restitution' and other politically correct terminology. That also means that restorative justice can be portrayed as a soft, liberal, 'Christian' option, favouring the offender in some notional balance, as against the victim. That delusion then allows even the well-intentioned sentencer to use sentences that are self-fulfilling in their retributive effect by making it almost impossible to allow healing and restoration other than as a strictly limited exercise conducted by well-meaning people with well-meaning people in spite of, rather than assisted by, a sensible sentence.

Restorative justice brings an alternative to the way we are responding to crime. Hebrew community manifestation of justice was an expression of restoring wholeness. 'Shalom' is more than the absence of conflict: it signifies completeness, fulfilment, wholeness – the existence of right relationships among individuals, the community and God. Crime was understood to break shalom, destroying right relationships within a community and creating harmful ones.

The concept of 'social sin' that departs from God's creation is a collective responsibility that demonstrates there is sin because humans create unjust situations that take away people's lives and opportunities to have access to medical services, education, shelter, food and jobs. The theological framework is taken from Gandhi, who warned against the 'seven social sins'. These can be characterized as politics without principle, wealth without work, commerce without morality, pleasure without conscience, education without character, science without humanity, and worship without sacrifice. Restorative justice can deal not simply with the symptoms but with the roots of problems that our political and economic systems create.

what is restorative justice?

The idea of restorative justice as the core concept of justice has several components: an insistence on the intrinsic value of all those affected by conflict or crime; the notion of crime as a disruption of the social fabric of a group or community; and a commitment to reconciliation as the path to just solutions to the harm done. Each of these components offers an alternative to the individualistic model of crime and justice now practised in England. Instead of seizing an individual accused by the state and defined by a criminal act, restorative justice gathers all who are affected by a criminal act. Instead of returning an indictment that satisfies rules of jurisprudence and prosecutorial practice, restorative justice views crime as an event in a specific location, an event with history and context. Instead of punishment as a moral or instrumental imposition on an individual, restorative justice seeks understanding of the harms and aspires to mend the separation brought about by conflict and crime.

The concept of restorative justice has inspired enthusiastic discussion, debate and commitment from individuals and groups from widely differing backgrounds. The vision of restorative justice can evoke strong emotional responses and differing views of community and reparation. This new presentation of a venerable idea of justice unites people in churches, in community groups and, increasingly, in government circles, in sentencers at every level, and creates excitement among critical criminologists, liberals and conservatives.

The locus of restoration is a dynamic and genuinely healing interchange between victim and offender. The emphasis often given by justice agencies to reparation is sadly misguided and unproductive. There is currently a debate about whether restorative justice is best served by implementation within or through state criminal justice agencies or outside of them. Experiments of both sorts are continuing and the current development of a strategy by the Government has provided an opportunity rarely available with such a major cultural issue. The tension in seeking to work with these ideas is evident from the work of Ruth Morris,[5] who recognized that the term restorative justice could be bent to the demands of those who would constrain what was to be restored or who envisioned a return to the inequalities that led to the conflict. She called for the use of the term 'transformative justice', to underscore the creative potential of reconciliation. It is not that we have had justice as society, lost it and that somehow it may be restored, but that we reach for justice and work at it, as the horizon recedes. Her caution in her address to the Canadian Criminal Justice Association in October 1997 put it more bluntly: 'the very principles of restorative justice risk becoming fundamentally distorted when the criminal justice system co-opts them; that is, when dynamic principles of transformation become mere management techniques in the hands of an essentially punitive justice system'. This warning should help inform the current consultation with the Government.

a definition of restorative justice

Restorative justice is a process whereby:

1. All parties with a stake in a particular conflict or offence come together to resolve collectively how to deal with the aftermath of the conflict or offence and its implications for the future.

2. Offenders have the opportunity to acknowledge the impact of what they have done and to make reparation, and victims have the opportunity to have their harm acknowledged and amends made.

Another version, from the Restorative Justice Consortium, reads:

> Restorative justice seeks to balance the concerns of the victim and the community with the need to reintegrate the offender into society. It seeks to assist the recovery of the victim and enable all parties with a stake in the justice process to participate fruitfully in it.[6]

There are other definitions and some of these are very wide, including such things as community service and victim awareness work with offenders. One guideline suggested by Helen Reeves of Victim Support is that an approach can only be deemed restorative if it attempts to put things right for victims.[7]

Restorative justice can thus be seen as a philosophical and programmatic alternative to the goals and procedures that characterize the present criminal system. There is a set of principles behind the practice that infuses its applications as well as a fast-developing set of practices (described in the Appendix). The principal site for restorative justice is not a court of law, nor a prison cell. It is a mediated encounter between those directly involved or affected by the crime: the victim, the offender, family members, and community representatives. The aim of these encounters is to facilitate:

- Transformation: where the individuals and communities concerned experience some degree of liberation from the conditions that perpetuate the cycle of violence, aggression, and domination exemplified in criminal behaviour; for example, by overcoming the negative emotions of fear and hatred, and by advancing the alleviation of various forms of degradation, oppression and stigmatization that characterize socio-political structures and interpersonal relations.
- Reconciliation: where the victim and offender – in the social rituals of apology and forgiveness – offer and receive the value and respect owed through their intrinsic human dignity and worth and engage in mutual condemnation of the criminal act, whilst casting off the offender's deviant or blameworthy status.

As a consequence of the above two being achieved, then it is possible to move to the third element of the process.

- Reparation: where the offender takes due responsibility for the crime by 'making good' the material harm done to the victim: that is by agreeing to provide a fair and mutually acceptable form of restitution and/or compensation.

The theory of restorative justice centres its challenge to the current justice system on the internal problem of the theory of retributive justice. Most retributivists are occupied by attempts to implement the idea of 'just deserts' within the current system. There is no description of what punishments feel like, how much they hurt, the suffering and the sorrow experienced by the prisoner, the harmful effects that his or her imprisonment may have on family and loved ones. The restorative view stresses that a theory of justice must show that its values and normative prescriptions might be successfully implemented in this world, in this socio-economic context, with this set of educational, race and gender inequalities, in this politically driven bureaucracy. In abstraction, the retributivist principle of deserved punishments is beautifully simple and compelling. But, as soon as someone tries to provide a map of how the principle might be embodied in social and experiential reality, one is faced with criminals who never fit the model of the rational, autonomous individual; and the imposition of punishment never quite seems to leave the sharp-edged impression that the human suffering and pain inflicted on the individual is precisely what he or she deserved.

It is in its self-conscious attempt to ensure that its core values are indeed situated in social and experiential reality that the theory of restorative justice transcends the retributivist theory. The human dimensions therefore involved in the operational objectives of restorative justice demand the highest quality of programme design and staff training. It is through the dynamics of interaction that victim and offender create a restitution agreement or perform the rituals of apology and forgiveness, or liberate each other from their stigmatized statuses of 'victim' or 'offender'. We do not yet know enough about the mystery of this process and should research it more.

reintegrative shaming

A helpful theory of restorative justice, which shows its critical difference from our traditional approach, is that of reintegrative shaming,[8] in which John Braithwaite argues for a restorative process of crime prevention that first makes clear to the offender that his or her behaviour is not condoned within the community; and then is respectful of the individual while not condoning the behaviour. It is this process that allows for a change in attitude and behaviour to take place. In other words, in the context of important and meaningful social relationships, attitude change towards a community can occur through an individual's taking responsibility for a wrongful act. This process allows reintegration to occur and subsequent acts of wrongdoing to be reduced. It has been labelled reintegrative shaming because the shaming is reintegrative rather than stigmatizing. Some proponents misunderstand this vital distinction, and regard shaming in itself as a positive factor in conditioning human behaviour. In doing so, they miss the point that shaming actually indicates that the person is inherently 'bad', whereas, by contrast, an emphasis on guilt points to the 'bad act' of an essentially good person. In fact, as Braithwaite's theory argues, shaming of a stigmatizing nature often results in further wrongful acts, because no change in attitude or behaviour has been expected or encouraged.

government strategy

The Government has published a consultation document on its strategy on restorative justice, *Restorative Justice: The Government's Strategy*,[9] which aims to maximize the use of restorative justice in the criminal justice system where the Government knows it works well to meet victims' needs and reduce reoffending. The Government also wants to encourage more high quality, visible reparation by offenders to the community.

Evidence suggests that restorative justice can help deliver key objectives across the criminal justice system: improving victim satisfaction, reducing crime and reoffending, delivering justice effectively and building public confidence. Many victims say they are interested in this approach and most who choose to participate in it are glad they did. Research shows it can also cut reoffending, particularly for more serious offenders.

The Government strategy has two elements. First the Government should build in high quality restorative justice at all stages of the criminal justice system by:

- putting restorative cautioning by the police on a statutory basis, as part of the new conditional cautioning introduced by the Criminal Justice Bill;
- developing a pilot scheme to test restorative justice as a diversion from prosecution;
- using the Criminal Justice Bill to make reparation a purpose of sentencing, and to make clear that reparative activities as part of sentencing can include victim-offender contact;
- setting out action to improve the delivery of restorative justice and reparation by the prison and probation services and looking at the role of restorative justice processes in case management;
- building on progress in the youth justice system, and building restorative justice into new developments in the adult justice system, such as intermittent custody centres and community justice centres;

- increasing understanding among professionals and the general public;
- developing a consistent approach to effective practice, training and accreditation for restorative justice practitioners, and enabling information sharing between agencies.

Second, the Government should develop its understanding of where restorative justice works best and how it could be fully integrated with the criminal justice system in the longer term, by further research and by developing policy on key issues about mainstreaming restorative justice in the criminal justice system.

The process of consultation and implementation provides the potential for a major change in approach in the experience of many victims and offenders in the future and is to be welcomed as a serious attempt to introduce a more inclusive approach to delivering justice.

international experience

There are many examples of restorative principles being used in national and international conflict resolution. Tribunals used at Nuremberg, in Yugoslavia, Rwanda, Cambodia and East Timor all have elements of seeking to establish the truth of what happened and, through this process, to enable people to move on after a decision about what should happen was made openly. These outcomes have included amnesty, the removal from power of those responsible for actions, compensation to victims and, in Canada, a public apology to the First Nations people for the damage inflicted on them in the past.

There are some 23 Truth and Reconciliation Commissions that have worked to achieve understanding and peace between peoples. The international example of restorative process most referred to is that of the Truth and Reconciliation Commission of South Africa where, in exchange for amnesty, those who had committed harm in the days of apartheid were enabled to tell their story so that those affected by the trauma were able to learn for the first time what had happened to their loved ones. There are countless examples of forgiveness being expressed through this process and many whose lives have been transformed by the experience. There remains much still to do in achieving a wider acceptance, and the continuing presence of local Peace Committees is continuing this vital work.

Desmond Tutu, who was part of the Truth and Reconciliation Commission in South Africa, has written:

> I contend that there is another kind of justice, restorative justice, which was the characteristic of traditional African jurisprudence. Here the central concern is not retribution or punishment but, in the spirit of *ubuntu*, the healing of breaches, the redressing of imbalances, and the restoration of broken relationships. This kind of justice seeks to rehabilitate both the victim and the perpetrator, who should be given the opportunity to be reintegrated into the community he or she has injured by his or her offence. This is a far more personal approach, which sees the offence as something that has happened to people and whose consequence is a rupture in relationships. Thus we would claim that justice, restorative justice, is being served when efforts are made to work for healing, for forgiveness and for reconciliation.[10]

criticisms and limitations

Restorative practice has difficulties because of the sensitivity of motivation and dynamics. Using the principles behind the process, it may be possible to overcome these limitations but they should be mentioned in this context. The criticisms involve assertions that:

- Restorative justice erodes legal rights. When guidelines and standards are maintained this does not happen. Part of the concern results from the experience that restorative practice has developed from the bottom up. Quite rightly, the rights of all involved are now closely considered in principles adhered to in practice. It cannot be said that current systems always adequately protect victims' and offenders' rights.
- Restorative justice results in net widening. Practice originally did concentrate on minor offences as access was available at that level, but current experience is that restorative processes should be aimed at the more persistent and serious offenders, given the practicality of limited resources and the potential in such cases for victims, offenders and communities to receive considerable benefits.
- Restorative justice trivializes crime. The experience of those involved in the process is that it takes crime more seriously because it focuses on the consequences of the offence for victims and attempts to address these and to find meaningful ways of holding offenders accountable.

- Restorative justice fails to 'restore' victims and offenders. Although we have referred to the uncertainty about this aspect earlier and to Ruth Morris's[11] preference in referring to the process as transformative, nevertheless, victims often feel that their security, dignity and a sense of control are restored. Offenders feel a sense of restoring responsibility to themselves for their offending and its consequences, restoring a sense of control to themselves to make amends for what they have done and restoring a belief in themselves that the processes were fair and just.
- Restorative justice fails to effect real change. The work is still at an early stage in many countries. However, in New Zealand there has been longer experience, and significant changes have occurred in the youth justice system so that far fewer young offenders appear in court and fewer young offenders are in custody (in 1989 there were 1,295; in 1992 it reduced to 655 and in 2001 there were 75). There are many research studies that show a real reduction in reoffending rates for more serious and personal offences.
- Restorative justice results in discriminatory outcomes. Affluent communities are more likely to develop the resources to support restorative processes but, if the programme has been implemented with statutory backing, access is open to all.
- Restorative justice encourages vigilantism. When it is equated with community or popular justice, there can be an association with repressive attitudes, but those are at odds with the values of restorative justice and cannot be part of it. Oversight by courts can be introduced to support community processes. Much vigilantism is in practice a response to perceived inadequacies of the conventional justice processes and sanctions.
- Restorative justice requires an accused or convicted person to admit guilt. This thus excludes from its processes those who, though found guilty, are, in fact, innocent; or at least those who protest their innocence despite forensic evidence to the contrary. Even when the innocent are found, on review, to have been victims of a miscarriage of justice, restorative justice processes become difficult, if not impossible.

However, there are many reasons to feel encouraged at the way in which developments in restorative justice are meeting the needs of communities, victims and offenders and helping them to take responsibility for their futures. What has the conventional criminal justice system achieved in the past decade that provides the same hope?

spiritual background to restorative processes

Traditionally there are four ways to move on from sinfulness: confession, pardon, penance and restoration to community. Restorative justice brings all these features into play through its processes and pathways to community:

1. the pathway of communication: listening and speaking and being wholly present to the other

2. the pathway of accountability: in honesty, speaking, sharing, and calling to account those responsible for acts that fracture the community

3. the pathway from shame to reintegration or welcome: compassionately allowing for second (third and fourth) chances and providing support and encouragement along the way

4. the pathway of forgiveness: having listened, holding each other accountable, welcoming each other within community, we now walk the path of forgiveness, open to the next person we meet along the way.

The chaos of our lives can become more understood through the power of forgiveness. We must distinguish between the need to forgive the person who has wounded us and the obligation to condemn what the person has done. The balance between these opposing values is vital. We must reclaim the future by forgiving offenders, by refusing to let their actions simply freeze time at a moment of passion or madness but, at the same time, we must retain the moral ability to identify the actions themselves as bad, as things that should never have been done.

What happens when restorative justice works has been described by Conrad Brunk:

> . . . offenders, victims, families, mediators, judges and lawyers who participate all speak of the 'magic', or 'deeply spiritual' aspects of the events which take place when offenders come to terms with the pain they have inflicted on victims or their families and express repentance, and when victims of crime or their families experience personal healing from offenders' acts of repentance and from their own ability to forgive.[12]

In Grendon Prison the therapeutic experience for the most serious violent and sexual offenders depended upon opportunities they took to educate themselves, increasing their self-worth through learning to be accountable and thereby enabling their enormous energy to express itself in positive, artistic and pro-social ways. They applied to join the community because they had reached a point at which they wanted to alter the pattern of their behaviour and themselves. Through brutally honest group sessions and community meetings the men acknowledged and owned the reality of the terrible things they had done, while at the same and without turning it into an excuse, they had to recognize that they themselves had been moulded by circumstances that were not in their control. What made the difference, what gave them back their future, was the decision to try to take control over their destiny, probably for the first time in their lives. Part of the process involved a radical kind of self-forgiveness that meant accepting the way the universe had formed them. This is dynamic forgiveness in action, but contained the drama of the offender's own life. Creative forgiveness can have a life-changing impact on all the actors in the tragedies of humanity.

Being unable to forgive can end up dominating a whole life or a life of a whole people. We can see this in international affairs as well as in the individual lives of victims.[13]

The parable of the Prodigal Son clearly shows the power of forgiveness. Some kind of order is introduced from the chaos of the irresponsible actions that cannot be undone. We are wired for retributive responses and it was to put things in order that Moses created laws of proportionate response in Exodus 21. Jesus replaced the sane and carefully calibrated response to injustice with a system of non-resistance. This is shown clearly in Jesus' words in Matthew 5, the Sermon on the Mount. 'Don't try to work out the proportionate response, move on, and let it go. Don't let resentment hijack your whole life. Turning the other cheek can be of immense strength.'

The father in the parable ran to his son and, in so doing, caused a true change in his son, forgiveness unconditionally given actually caused the repentance that followed: 'Father, I have sinned against heaven and before you; I am no longer worthy to be called your son' (Luke 15.21).

Henri Nouwen in *The Return of the Prodigal Son*,[14] comments on the painting of Rembrandt on this subject.

> The longer I look at 'the patriarch' the clearer it becomes to me
> that Rembrandt has done something quite different from letting God

pose as the wise old head of the family. It all begins with the hands. The two are quite different. The father's left hand touching the son's shoulder is strong and muscular. The fingers are spread out and cover a large part of the prodigal son's shoulder and back. I can see a certain pressure, especially in the thumb. That hand seems not only to touch, but, with its strength, also to hold. Even though there is a gentleness in the way the father's left hand touches his son, it is not without a firm grip.

How different is the father's right hand! This hand does not hold or grasp. It is refined, soft, and very tender. The fingers are close to each other and have an elegant quality. It lies gently upon the son's shoulder. It wants to caress, to stroke, and to offer consolation and comfort. It is a mother's hand . . .

As soon as I recognised the difference between the two hands of the father, a new world of meaning opened up for me. The father is not simply a great patriarch. He is mother as well as father. He touches the son with a masculine hand and a feminine hand. He holds, she caresses. He confirms and she consoles. He is, indeed, God, in whom both manhood and womanhood, fatherhood and motherhood, are fully present.

Spiritual traditions see justice and truth as relational concepts developed in a universe underpinned by a moral order. Human identity can only be understood in the context within which human beings 'live, move and have their being'. According to an Aboriginal phrase, life is about 'all my relations'. That phrase is used when commencing and ending prayers and discussions as a sign of deference and respect towards the totality of life throughout all time and place, as well as to the community to which it is addressed.

My experience of being welcomed into a 'sweat lodge' in a prison on Vancouver Island was of an intense awareness of the closeness with others in the womb-like silence of the gathering of prisoners and guests. The leadership of the elder was shared with others in the group who had roles in developing the safety of the setting, so that all felt respected and could feel the power of being together in communion. 'All my relations' in action.

The Christian way is pre-eminently restorative, for Jesus preached the revolutionary ethic of forgiveness, non-violence, reconciliation and love for each human individual. Restorative justice, with its principles of repentance, forgiveness and reconciliation is a deeply spiritual process. It is never an easy way out; neither for the offender, the victim, nor the community. It requires all of us to come to grips with who we are, what we have done, and what we can become in the fullness of our humanity. It is about doing justice as if people really mattered, and addresses the need for a vision of the good life, and the common good.

The experience of The Spiritual Roots Project from the Centre for Studies in Religion and Society at the University of Victoria[15] leads us to a wider vision of justice in a global setting where the boundaries between cultures are blurred. Faith communities have more to contribute to harmony than conflict and, through restorative justice, there is a process concerned with healing the wounds of victim, offender and community alike.

the value of persons

> Brotherhood in most of the myths I know of is confined to a bounded community. In bounded communities, aggression is projected outward. For example, the Ten Commandments say, 'Thou shalt not kill.' Then the next chapter says, 'Go into Canaan and kill everybody in it.' This is a bounded field. The myths of participation and love pertain only to the in-group, and the out-group is totally other. This is the sense of the word 'gentile' – the person is not of the same order.[16]

The concept of bounded fields is very important in our thinking about justice. In most religious traditions the value given to insiders differs from that given to outsiders. The result is what could be called boundary thinking, in which humans are valued differently depending on whether they belong to my group or another, whether they are insiders or outsiders, of my tribe or another.

Restorative justice is premised on the assumption that all humans are of intrinsic value – whether insider or outsider. But, if Campbell is correct, we cannot assume that this is accepted even in religious communities. Indeed, religious communities, which hold strongly to a core of beliefs and values, are easily tempted to deprecate the intrinsic value of those beyond their borders who believe, think and act differently. We see evidence of this in religious communities around the world.

And it is not new. Boundary thinking, in this sense of valuing humans differently, was prevalent at the time of Jesus and he constantly exploded such thinking – whether in reference to Gentiles, Samaritans, prostitutes, children, women, tax collectors or the two criminals who hung on the crosses on either side of him as he and they died together.

Boundary thinking of this nature is a challenge for us today. Restorative justice is more likely to become a compelling option if the communities in which we live, religious or otherwise, will first become convinced that all humans have such worth that the great energy and time and resources required to do the work of restorative justice are worth the effort. For Christian communities, this is the imperative that Jesus has set forth. For all communities, it is the model most likely to lead to personal and societal wholeness and health.

William Blake's 'The Everlasting Gospel'[17] is prefaced by a prose paragraph that considers the originality of Jesus' teaching on forgiveness. In response to Peter's question about the frequency of forgiving, in saying 'seventy times seven' Jesus has told us never to stop forgiving: 'For if you forgive others their trespasses, your heavenly Father will also forgive you; but if you do not forgive others, neither will your Father forgive your trespasses' (Matthew 6.14-15).

It seems that forgiveness awaits reciprocal movement on the part of men and women. The parable of the Prodigal Son might more truly be called the parable of the Forgiving Father. Asking and accepting forgiveness releases the capacity to love: 'Her sins, which were many, have been forgiven; hence she has shown great love' (Luke 7.47).

Forgiveness releases love for service. Forgiveness makes possible a deeper communion than that which existed before. It is of cosmic proportion.

The world reached a new level of raised consciousness and nobility of spirit when Jesus uttered from the cross the words, 'Father, forgive them, for they do not know what they are doing' (Luke 23.34).

appendix

restorative processes and mediation in the criminal justice system

Restorative justice can take place in the criminal justice system at all stages (provided the offender acknowledges responsibility, and the victim is willing):

- through diversion to community or school mediation;
- through diversion at arrest by police;
- between conviction and sentencing;
- post-sentence, in the community, in prison or when released;
- during the duration of the sentence, whether in prison, in half-way houses, or on parole.

applications of restorative justice

victim–offender mediation

This is the process in which an impartial third party helps the victim(s) and offender(s) to communicate, either directly or indirectly. The mediation process can lead to greater understanding for both parties and sometimes to tangible reparation.

reparation

This is the action taken by the offender(s) to put right the harm done, whether directly to the victim or indirectly to the community.

victim–offender conferencing

This is similar in principle to victim–offender mediation but involves families of victims and offenders, and other relevant members of the community.

family group conferencing

Similar to victim–offender conferencing but the offender's family has some private time to come up with a viable plan for reparation and for the future.

victim–offender groups

These are groups in which victims of crime and offenders meet, usually for a set number of sessions, where the victims have suffered similar crimes (but not the actual crimes) to those perpetrated by the offenders.

current developments

New legislation in the UK provides some specific opportunities for restorative approaches to be used.

Crime and Disorder Act 1998

This Act set up youth offending teams in each area of England and Wales, bringing together police, social workers, probation officers, and health and education workers. It also provides a role for victim awareness work, mediation, reparation and conferencing in the following provisions:

final warning

This is usually given for a second minor offence, following a reprimand for a first minor offence. After a final warning, the young person must be referred to the local youth offending team for a rehabilitation programme, to prevent re-offending. This can include victim awareness work, mediation or reparation.

reparation order

This requires young offenders to make reparation to the victim or to the community. It can involve up to 24 hours' work and must be completed within three months. It does not include monetary compensation. Victim awareness work, mediation and reparation work can all count towards the hours of a reparation order. Victims need time to consider whether they would like direct reparation, and it is important that they are not under any pressure to take part. If they do not want to take part, community reparation will be more appropriate, and many community organizations can be involved.

action plan orders

This order requires a young offender to follow an action plan for three months, which can include a variety of activities designed to prevent further offending. These activities are specified in the order and can include victim awareness, mediation or reparation.

supervision orders

A supervision order provides supervision of a young offender for a period of time (often one or two years). These orders have existed for many years, but the Crime and Disorder Act makes provision for them to include mediation and reparation where appropriate.

Youth Justice and Criminal Evidence Act 1999

This provides a new sentence for 10- to 17-year-olds pleading guilty and convicted for the first time.

referral orders

The referral order involves referral of the young person to a youth offender panel, which meets in an informal setting away from the court. The people involved in this meeting are the young person, their family, the victims if they wish (but there is no pressure to attend), a member of the youth offending team (which is responsible for preparations for the meeting) and two panel members drawn from the local community (and provided with training for this work), one of whom chairs the panel meeting. Other relevant people may also attend, such as a teacher from the young person's school.

The meeting considers the circumstances leading to the offending behaviour and the effect of the crime on the victim. The panel then agrees a contract with the young person, including reparation to the victim or to the wider community, and a programme of activity designed primarily to prevent further offending. The aim of the referral order is for the young person to accept responsibility for his or her offending behaviour and to consider – along with those with a positive influence over the young person – how to deal with the causes. The offence becomes 'spent' as soon as the order has been completed.

local initiatives

It is left up to local youth offending teams to find their own way of implementing these provisions. In some teams, all staff are involved in restorative work, in others a specialist restorative justice worker takes on this responsibility. In many areas, youth offending teams work together with a local mediation service that already has trained volunteer mediators.

restorative justice in schools

The ideas of restorative justice are being transferred to schools, in two government-backed projects and by many other initiatives. Processes involved can include peer mediation, circle time, mediation to avoid school exclusion and reorientating the whole disciplinary system along restorative lines.

other related processes and services

There are several other processes and services, which, while not restoring victims directly, work to reduce the likelihood of more victims being created.

Alternatives to Violence Project (AVP)

This project takes conflict resolution workshops into prisons to offer prisoners alternative ways of responding to conflict situations, without violence.

circles of support and accountability for sex offenders

A small number of volunteers (4–6) are recruited from the community in which a high-risk sex offender will be living. A circle is a support network for the offender, while holding him accountable for his actions. These circles have been proved to cut the rate of reoffending of sex offenders in Canada and to help communities feel safer. Quakers in Britain manage a pilot scheme in the Thames Valley as well as supporting a scheme in Hampshire and one run by the Lucy Faithful Foundation.

community mediation services

These extensive services in most localities use mediation to defuse neighbour and community conflict, some of which could escalate into crime.

community chaplaincy services

Community resources are coordinated through chaplains locally based to support the sensitive process of prisoners' resettling in the community.

responsible sentencing

The work being undertaken by a team led by Stephen Pryor under the title 'The Responsible Sentence' proposes that the use of imprisonment should be made more specific by the courts when sentencing, drawing on the development of sentence planning as a system including the part to be served in the community. This concept inevitably includes the requirement that the courts' powers of punishment are used to repair the damage done to the social fabric by the offence. That means that the whole approach to the custodial sentence would favour restorative justice, however narrowly or broadly defined.

the benefits of restorative approaches

Through restorative practice **victims** have the opportunity to

- learn about the offender and put a face to the crime;
- ask questions of the offender;
- express their feelings and needs after the crime;
- receive an apology and/or appropriate reparation;
- educate offenders about the effects of their offences;
- sort out any existing conflict;
- be part of the criminal justice process;
- put the crime behind them;
- reduce their fear for the future.

Offenders have the opportunity to

- own the responsibility for their crime;
- find out the effect of their crime;
- apologize and/or offer appropriate reparation;
- reassess their future behaviour in the light of this knowledge;
- regain their place as citizens in a law-abiding society.

Courts have the opportunity to

- learn about victims' needs;
- make more realistic sentences;
- enable victims to participate in the criminal justice process;
- make significant provision to meet victims' needs.

Communities have the opportunity to

- accept apologies and reparation from offenders;
- help reintegrate victims and offenders;
- obtain lasting solutions to local conflicts;
- become safer through confidence-building, fostering trust.

chapter 3
responsible sentencing
Stephen Pryor

a prison system amok

To someone unfamiliar with the criminal justice process it may come as a surprise to learn that those responsible for the most expensive and most disabling sentence are largely unaccountable for what they do with the sentence. Prison governors receive no guidance or instruction from the courts. Prisoners are given no clue as to what is expected of them. Victims can only take pot luck as to whether they may expect there to be any connection between what they have suffered and what the offender might be required to do about it. And the taxpayer and voter are left in ignorance of how the system works to protect the community and why it costs so much.

This chapter shows how, by knowingly granting licence to prisons to remove responsibility from offenders in custody, and by ensuring that the courts have no jurisdiction to require prisons to use time in custody purposefully, society demonstrates a hypocrisy that ill serves victims and others damaged by crime. The chapter goes on to identify the peculiar responsibility of the Church to address this under the mandate Christ gave, that we fail to love him where we fail to love the prisoner. Perhaps we might recognize that injunction better if it were rephrased to read that our exclusion of the prisoner reflects our exclusion of Christ.

These claims and the language, including the word 'amok', are perhaps dramatic, and may offend by appearing to sweep much that is good and reforming away with what is agreed to be rotten. They may also be thought to lack realism. This chapter suggests that we cannot compromise.

It may be useful to understand how this idea took hold. It is a story worth telling. The author asks the reader's forgiveness as he moves from the third to the first person and he warms to his theme.

The author was a prison governor grade for 37 years, retiring in November 2001. In addition to governing a number of local (i.e. remand) prisons, he was asked to do a number of jobs in Prison Service Headquarters that required a fundamental questioning of the purpose and function of imprisonment. Two of these jobs, both in industrial relations, often revealed completely opposing views of the job of the prison officer – to obey orders or to think for him- or herself, to treat prisoners with humanity or to ensure that they were dehumanized sufficiently to accept the conditions of overcrowding and under-resourcing that often went with the job. A third, in the Suicide Awareness and Support Unit, now absorbed within Safer Custody, meant recognizing the prisoner as person, the family as family, and the truth as a commodity as valuable to the caring prison officer and governor as to the family and the listener.

On returning to the field, each year, in Prisoner Week, I held an event that took some theme out of its normal context and examined it from a moral or ethical (or sometimes both) perspective. (In this context 'moral' implies a spectrum of good to bad against some notion of truth, 'ethical' implies one stretching from right to wrong against some notion of what is socially acceptable, with some overlap between them.)

The year 1991 was very significant: I opened a new prison at High Down; the Woolf report on Strangeways was published,[1] with an emphasis on justice in prisons; the 1991 Criminal Justice Act, coming at a time of declining prison numbers, centred on proportionality in sentencing, encouraging the idea that we might see some method in the 'un-rationality' of sentencing. I formed an early partnership with the Geese Theatre Company, who taught prisoners to write and produce thought-provoking and highly amusing playlets.[2] Their first series was on the handling of Aids. That led me to ask if the men would consider doing the same on the theme of responsibility in prison. This they did, and they put on five little plays – very amusing and very accurately observed, with the full support of the magistrates and staff whom they caricatured.

In the first they showed how, at the point of arrest, the 'prisoner' lost much responsibility, and if he or she mistook that or felt like taking it as a laugh, would quickly learn their mistake. Anyone who had been arrested recognized that. When the 'prisoner' was charged, again, anyone who thought that the job of deciding if there was a prima facie case was left under no illusion what the police thought, and hence what others were likely to think too. Then came the appearance in court. Our Board of Visitors (now Independent Monitoring Board) Chairman, who was also the Chairman of the Local Bench, spoke very movingly of his new understanding of the power he used to enforce his authority over the 'defendant' through language, use of the courtroom, and expected behaviour.

The third playlet concerned reception into prison, which has been described so often that most people recognize the potency of the process, of giving up personal possessions, receiving institutional substitutes, and feeling terribly alone, and it comes as no surprise to learn that these first few days are the time of highest risk of suicide.

The last two playlets portrayed the process of institutionalization coming full circle. At the Sentence Review Board, the successful conformist received his ample reward, while the prisoner struggling with his inner soul was punished for apparently questioning the system, which could cope only with conformity. In the final scene, under the banner 'Howard's Way' (he was Home Secretary at the time), the Discharge Board showed the conformist walking, almost dancing, out of the gate arm in arm with the Governor. Then the man who had struggled to come to terms with his offence was kept until the eleventh hour, and kicked out of the gate on the stroke of midnight, when the lights went out.

Those scenes told two stories: that prisoners know the sacrifice expected of them to become prisoners; and that we, their gaolers, know they know.

If there is no violent rage to justify using the word 'amok' to describe the state of prisons, the reader might usefully reflect on Strangeways and ask what has changed to account for the acceptance of today's conditions.

To describe prisons as a system amok may be harsh. But to say that they simply behave without accountability for any requirement from the court, and that the experience of prisoners is one of an immensely variable and personal interpretation of what the community might want, would be to understate the position. Inspection reveals great variation, a seeming inability to learn from mistakes and spread good practice, and some appalling practice that no amount of shifting or disciplining of senior managers seems to cure. That we may have become more adept at persuading people of the wisdom of behaving as prisoners may be a tribute to our reasonableness and skills of persuasion, but the playlets reminded me that the prisoners may also be aware of the importance of the second stage, that the prisoner needs to return to being a citizen. If the violent rage is internalized, and the resulting frustration is shown by self-harm and fewer opportunities for earned responsibility and release, the fact that the Church is silent on the issue of un-responsible sentencing will not help to release the tension and despair.

The following section takes the story on to 2001.

The Responsible Prisoner and *Responsible Sentence* projects

With eight months left before retirement, I had completed one job, and there was no other plan for me. I therefore asked if I might explore the extent to which prisons removed responsibility unnecessarily, locating myself in the Prisons Inspectorate, where the information I needed was readily available. This was granted and I was made very welcome by Sir David Ramsbotham and his team. I contacted a number of people – a reference group of around 120 – from all kinds of interest groups, including the Prisons Ombudsman and Inspectors from different parts of the criminal justice system, and from within the prison service, including governors and prisoners old and young and of both sexes. Of particular significance in this context was the help and perspective given by Peter Sedgwick, whose knowledge, wisdom and location on the Board for Social Responsibility I had known for some years.

The full story is set out in my Report *The Responsible Prisoner – an exploration of the extent to which imprisonment removes responsibility unnecessarily*, published as I retired in November 2001, and still available on the Home Office and Prison Service web sites.[3]

At the heart of this study is a 30-question questionnaire, leading from the straightforward to the complex, and from first custody to post-release. Suffice to say here, the hypothesis that imprisonment involved far more removal of responsibility than was needed simply to protect the public and incapacitate the offender was strongly supported. Some governors rejected prisoners' having their own privacy locks because they could not trust them, while others – including all private prisons –already had them. These locks not only save staff time, and prevent cell thefts, they give a prisoner a sense of decency and privacy.

At the other end of the questionnaire, I asked what governors felt might be appropriate topics for consultation with prisoners – suggesting a range from diet and hobbies to safe staffing levels for control and security. Again some said it would be dangerous to lead prisoners to expect that they might influence the latter, while others said it could be dangerous to try to veto such discussions.

There were many fascinating insights along the way. Private prisons seemed relaxed about giving prisoners responsibility, regarding their relationship with prisoners as a sort of contract – prisoners got what the contract said they were entitled to, not what an individual might feel was their due. Prisons that gave prisoners responsible jobs to help to run the prison saved a lot of money and got a sense of ownership in return. Many governors said that they encouraged 'after-sales' support of prisoners following release, despite an order that said they should not; others quoted the order (and lack of resources) as the reason for not doing so. For every question there was a set of proposals drawing on what was actually happening in some part of the prison service.

It is perhaps worth stressing at this point that the author is not suggesting that in some way the experience of responsibility is good for offenders per se. That may be true for some; for some it may be that they already have too high a notion of their ability to take responsibility. And, as has subsequently been pointed out, many of the communities to which we belong discourage much in the way of initiative and taking responsibility. Certainly, as a governor, my job was to run a safe prison, and that often involved helping people to adapt to the role of prisoner, with all the tolerance and ambivalence that entails. Many of the opportunities to take responsibility in prison, for example the role of Listener, as trained by the Samaritans, are not easily replicated or compared with those outside. They need 'translation'. None of that takes anything away from giving and expecting responsibility. It only reinforces that we, that is to say society acting through the prison , should be careful not to take responsibility away unnecessarily, lest we do the one thing we try not to do, to make irresponsible people 'un-responsible', unable to take responsibility.

The work culminated in two conferences at Highpoint Prison, with men and women prisoners taking a full part. At the first we checked if our preliminary findings rang true with all present. At the second we reported back on what we had done about the findings.

After publication, a number of my reference group pointed out that the lack of any direction or guidance from the sentencer to the prison service, let alone any preliminary discovery of what a sentence plan might look like, or any commitment by the prison service to discharge a plan it had proposed or been required to perform by the court, was unhelpful when trying to frame a sensible, appropriate and 'seamless' sentence with other agencies. It also made it a matter of conjecture as to whether the prisoner him- or herself paid any attention to what others might think appropriate. And the victim was only one of many – perhaps including the judiciary – who had little idea of what a prison sentence might mean, or what scope there was for restorative justice.

I had some awareness of my ignorance of sentencing, and much more about the fast-flowing criminal justice agenda. But, against that, I knew that there was nothing to know about sensible sentencing, other than perhaps in the juvenile and youth offending sectors where there was a considerable investment in what I came to call a 'contract' sentence. In such a sentence the community (in the form of youth offending teams), the person being sentenced and the custodian are enjoined by the sentencer to carry out a fairly specific plan, involving a degree of involvement and commitment by the offender. There is even a small sanction on the custodian for non-delivery.

Whether or not that idea of a useful sentence has had anything to do with the continued increase in the young prison population is unknown to the author, but a similar increase in the adult female population and a lesser (albeit record) increase in the adult male population would suggest that the courts are voting for custody not out of confidence but out of despair, for a break if nothing else.

A particular characteristic of recent criminal justice policy and strategies has been the plethora of initiatives (and Acts). To that extent it is not easy to say that one is proposing something new, and, if so, only because it is new. The innovative inquiry on alternatives to custody, sponsored by the Esmée Fairbairn Foundation's offspring *Re-thinking Crime and Punishment* (RCP) inquiry, scopes many of them.[4] Whether any seriously examine the arguments for denying ourselves custody or for involving the prison service and the offender in the sentence is unknown at the time of writing. Certainly the Churches' Criminal Justice Forum – again with Peter Sedgwick and again under the sponsorship of RCP – is asking how the Church can contribute. And the many other initiatives such as *What Can I Do?* (another RCP and CCJF publication) show that there is no lack of recognition of the need for community involvement.[5]

The *Responsible Sentence* project is not complete at the time of writing, but its main conclusions are becoming clear. There is no link between the sentencer and the adult prison system. There is an IT mechanism in the form of OASys,[6] which has the potential to identify risk and how a sentence might tackle that risk across the boundary between custody and the community. There is a human rights agenda, which is increasingly questioning the right of the State to act arbitrarily against prisoners. There are fertile fields, of which the Thames Valley Partnership is one, for encouraging a culture of active citizenship, victim and community healing and devolved accountability embracing prisons, if only as passive containers. This (and not stamping down on antisocial behaviour) should be the focus for the new Home Office Centre for Active Citizenship. At the time of writing, the *Responsible Sentence* steering group is exploring with some Thames Valley Partnership and local Oxfordshire sentencers how the adult and Young Offender prisons might be brought in by the courts to play a more useful and appropriate part.

So much for stories. In the next section we look at the moral debate around responsible sentencing. It may be as well at this juncture to remind the reader where this is leading. What does Christ have to say, and what might that mean for the Church, and the Church in Parliament in particular?

the moral debate

The idea that people should lose no more responsibility than is necessary for their custody is over-simple. Few recognize that prisons are deliberately given wide licence in interpreting a sentence – and that this is for a perfectly sensible reason. As soon as the prison can assess the prisoner's reliability and risk to the public (and her- or himself), the level of control and security can be reduced. And often that assessment can be made very early on, often before the trial. And quite often that assessment will show that the justification for a prison sentence has nothing to do with risk. Indeed every governor loves lifers because they are the most sensible, mature, considerate and responsible prisoners you could hope to have on board.

There are powerful reasons for sending people to prison. They include the five statutory purposes proposed in the Bill (punishment, reduction of crime including deterrence, reform and rehabilitation, protection of the public and reparation) as well as making an example of offenders, sometimes protecting the offender, giving satisfaction to the victim, and pleasing the *Daily Mail* reader. Some may also feel that prisons have now become self-perpetuating such that the prisoning has become a major industry with an identifiable voter signature in America, and a growing one here.

But the most elusive, yet most powerful, reason for imprisoning – and the one that should concern churchmen and women, and any who call themselves Christian, is the one that allows us to cut our fellows off, to deny our neighbour, and dismiss Christ's injunction to love prisoners particularly, and particularly because what we do to them we do to him.

banishment

People recoil from that word. 'Incapacitating'? Well, that is, regrettably, essential for a hard core (but don't expect a consensus on that core). 'Segregation'? Well, that is sometimes the only way we can administer a necessary programme with any certainty of success, for example the Sex Offender Treatment programme – and in that case they probably have to be protected anyway. That conveniently ignores the fact that Vulnerable Prisoners as a distinct group did not exist a few years ago, and stand witness to a culture of hatred between prisoners before which prison managers have bowed.

Banishment has a long history. From the practice in classical times of putting people outside the known world, to transportation, to putting people 'away', or 'exclusion' as we refer to it today when not talking about imprisoning miscreants. Gone are the 'judges of gaol delivery' whose job was to empty the prisons on their circuit by 'oyer and terminer'. Perhaps they went the way of beheading and branding and other barbaric disposals, but they also gave way to imprisonment as a finite disposal. It is interesting to note in passing that forgiveness makes sound economic sense, that the money needed to lock people up (including the light custody of open and low-security prisons) is around £37,000 a year, and that quite respectable research shows that the public is not as vindictive as our political representatives would sometimes have themselves believe.

To take authority for locking up one's neighbour means waiving some important constraints on our moral and ethical licences. We – the courts, the prison service, society as a whole – all have to believe that imprisonment is necessary to protect the public. We have to believe that we can really protect the public by locking people up until it is safe to let them out. We have to believe that locking people up will make them better, or at least wiser. We have to believe not just that a bit of education and training, a bit of detoxification, is a decent thing to offer, but that it will actually help to prevent reoffending. We have to believe that, if we discover that a prison is treating people badly, we can stop that. And we have to show that prisons represent value for money as a means of making the community safe and the offender law-abiding and useful.

The trouble is, and it is a particular trouble for church people, that prisons allow Christians and other good people to do good. They allow us to have pity and to take it. Without prisons there could be no prison reform, no Prison Visitors or Prison Fellowship, no moral repugnance, no ethical misgivings, no issues of multi-faith. And, of course, no prisoners. That we have only invented prison quite recently allows us to think fairly freely about what else we have set up to maintain a humane prison system. But it may also blind us to the underlying hatred or indifference that prompted us to sanctify them in the first place.

A small parallel may help. Until a year or two ago the prison service had not identified prisoners needing protection as being 'vulnerable'. They were segregated on Rule 43, roughly according to the space we made available: 12 for Londoners north of the Thames in Wormwood Scrubs, and 426 in Wandsworth G, H and K wings for those south of the river. Signing them on every month was a meaningless chore for the (then) Board of Visitors. It was easier to think of them as enjoying a full regime, but separate, and to redesignate G, H and K wings as a Vulnerable Prisoner Unit. And it was ideal to co-locate many who were hated for their sex offence so that we could run a Sex Offender Treatment Programme on one site. So we used a culture of prisoner hatred to administer a key programme. If the prisoners had tolerated, even loved one another, or if the Governor had taken a tough line on the haters (as did the then Governor of Lancaster Farms which, though doing the same job as Feltham, used bullies to tackle bullying and had no segregated or vulnerable youngsters), we would have had some difficulty in organizing suitable programmes.

The Church must have a view on the issues that prison raises. What does overcrowding denote? What does a major rise in the custody of women and youngsters denote? What is the importance of penitence and forgiveness in sentencing? How right is the involvement of the victim in sentencing and parole? By what right do we deny some lifers any hope of release? And how do we, particularly but not exclusively Christians, demonstrate our love and inclusion of offenders throughout the sentencing process?

how the prison service copes

One of the interesting things about the dimension of responsibility is its neutrality. Holding an offender responsible for his or her sentence is a reasonable and ethical thing to do. But it has no moral dimension. Refusing to accept responsibility for one's acts, on the other hand, or for righting the wrong, or simply for making society a better place to have one's being, is rightly condemned on moral and ethical grounds. And refusing to require responsibility, or, worse, refusal to allow it, is the same.

Prisons are allowed to refuse responsibility. They are answerable to no one for their risk assessment – unless they allow too wide a latitude, as judged by their political masters. No minister was ever embarrassed by keeping a prisoner in.

Sentencers are allowed to refuse responsibility. Not only do they refuse it to prisons, they do so to prisoners, at least to adult prisoners. No judge can give an order to a governor other than to 'hold' a prisoner. Thus no sentence has a declared purpose, other than to hold for a specified outer limit of time. We may hope that the Bill will make this a requirement, or at least recognized as good practice. That outer limit never means what it says. A twelve-month sentence usually means twelve weeks before release on the tag. 'Life' has two meanings or levels of seriousness, depending on whether it resulted from 'two-strikes' or something worse.

Because the prison sentence is never required to make sense it is hardly surprising if, sometimes, the probation service, which is expected to pick up the sentence mid-term, may find the course of custody rather puzzling. It would not be unreasonable also if the offender were to question a sentence plan that seemed to have more to do with prison performance, and filling slots, than with his or her needs or those of the victim or the community.

This is not fanciful. But it casts a fanciful veil over some of our ways of thinking of a sentence.

Restorative justice is very sensible and worthwhile, if hard work and rather patchy in application. That the prison service can sometimes organize restorative justice conferences in prisons, and through them achieve sometimes astonishing restoration must not be confused with the rightness of custody or the desirability of the penitence of the prisoner. What may come to light is the wrongness of custody, the twist of the adversarial process and the need for a balance of responsibility between the offender and the victim as fellow-members of their various communities.

That serving prisoners help over 1,000 Citizens Advice clients each every year – as they do in the OXCAB–Springhill partnership – says nothing good about their sentence.[7] It was not the second sight of the judge in giving them such colossal sentences. It was not any visionary sentence planner. It was not even any desire of the prisoner. It has never been mentioned in the same breath as restorative justice. It was simply the result of asking what competent people in prison might do to meet the shortfall in helping clients, 19 out of 20 of whom could not even get through on the phone.

That it works has little to do with the parent organizations, which might well switch it off if it got bad publicity, despite the help being given to very needy people.

Once we invented prison as a determinate sentence, we had to invent a whole set of rules that only make sense in that nonsensical context. There is nothing really sensible about the length of a sentence other than as an indicator of disapproval by tariff. Efforts to introduce standardization often result in the median being taken for the entry point. A sentence served in an open prison near home might not be a great hardship for a competent sophisticate with a good family and plenty of money, by comparison with one served by a woman drug mule half a world away from her family, locked up in closed conditions because it would be unseemly for someone with her offence to enjoy open conditions.

This is not fanciful.

Defendants are not asked how they would propose to repair the damage done by their offence: were they to suggest it, they would be ignored or told to stop trying to wriggle out of their responsibility, when facing it, or coming to terms with it may be exactly what they are trying to do.

There seems to be no one able to overarch the two worlds. One holds that convicted offenders forgo any claim to responsibility by their offence. The other holds that convicted offenders should not be excused responsibility, and the sooner they face it and grow up the sooner they can take on active citizenship. Removing the vote is about as silly as it gets, though there are far worse penalties if one looks at the fate of prisoners' families, the dangers in prison, and how else one might spend £37,000 times 75,000 every year.

the judgement of Christ

What should the Church say, following the example of Christ?

Let us go back to the concept of banishment as directly contrary to Christ's command that we love one another, particularly prisoners. That command should lie at the core of Christian thinking about criminal justice and sentencing, and it bears steady reinforcement so that we do not allow ourselves to slip into rationalization of what may be expedient or smart. It should also serve as a test for non-Christian sentence models.

If anyone said something important about victims, it was Christ. He said we should be very careful about judging to finality. He said we should never give up on offenders. He chose to die as a criminal. Praying for our enemy is to give him or her a responsibility that an adversarial trial cannot. Necessary though it is to have no reasonable doubt as to guilt, even certainty does not allow us to remove responsibility. Indeed, the more certain we are, the more care we have to take to protect, and reasonably to assume, responsibility.

Forgiveness is Christian. It also makes a lot of sense, and is considerably cheaper than banishment. But according responsibility is not the same as forgiveness. Just as a responsible sentence – one that requires the prison service along with all other agencies and the community to require and recognize responsibility as the basis for restoring the social fabric through sentencing – provides a helpful context for restorative justice, so it encourages forgiveness and repentance. 'I find it hard not to let contrition melt my heart' said a judge in the early stages of the project. But responsible sentencing can take place without restorative justice or forgiveness.

What is different is that, without responsible sentencing, no one can say that they have fulfilled Christ's command that we love our neighbour. No one can love those they have put away. And we put people away when we put them in prison without a purpose.

The Church has difficulties in this debate. It would say that we should be nice to prisoners. It would say that we should not insist on penance and forgiveness in case we upset other faiths. It would say that the size of the prison population is not a matter for the Church's concern and condemnation, only the resulting conditions. And, of course, there may be more straightforward disasters abroad that deserve our attention.

But who other than the Church will say that we are abandoning offenders when we imprison them? That we are denying them their civil rights far beyond what is necessary to prevent their offending? That we are not even asking ourselves, let alone them or the agencies or their community, or the victim where there is one, how best we can use the power of the sentence and the authority of the court to make good?

And who would challenge the Church's authority to speak about what is good?

chapter 4

the churches
and criminal justice

Stuart Dew

I spend a good deal of time trying to press upon churches the notion that the criminal justice system, and those who fall foul of it, should be a cause for Christian concern. It still surprises me – although perhaps, by now, it shouldn't – that this is not always as glaringly obvious to others as it is to me.

There are many reasons why churchgoing Christians might not put criminal justice top of their list of concerns. Some may see the subject as too political, or too radical, while some may feel safer supporting a mission field far from home. Others may make a simple distinction between the deserving and the undeserving – with offenders being regarded as undeserving because of their offences – failing to separate the sinner from the sin.

The truth is that the law, and those who come into conflict with it, has been a prominent focus within Christianity from the very beginning. The thrust of Christ's earthly ministry was to those who, daily, clog our courts, prisons and probation offices. He engaged the cheat, the robber, the beggar and the prostitute. He had time for the mentally ill, others whom nice folks avoided, and those not quite able to make their way in the world. And, of course, he experienced for himself the harshness of the justice system at the time. He was arrested in the middle of the night on the word of a friend who was a paid informer, subjected to intimidating questioning and remanded in custody. He was subjected to police brutality, and condemned to die by a weak judge who was put under pressure by the prosecution.[1]

(Incidentally, the Bible also gives a glimpse of how different things might be, with the imprisonment of the Apostle Paul suggesting an Elysian custodial environment in which inmates and staff show touching concern for one another. An earthquake occurs, the prison doors burst open, and the terrified jailer is about to commit suicide, fearing that his charges have escaped. Paul stops him from harming himself and, in a reciprocal gesture, the jailer washes the wounds of Paul and Silas (Acts 16.25-34).)

Often, the great prison reformers of the eighteenth and nineteenth centuries who sought to make our prisons more humane, were driven by a faith conviction. Elizabeth Fry, who came from a wealthy Quaker family, was encouraged to visit the women's yard at Newgate Prison by a family friend and immediately became a tireless campaigner for reform. She founded the first prison school, at Newgate, in 1817, seeing – as we still struggle to get some to see today – the importance of constructive prison regimes.

John Howard, after whom the Howard League for Penal Reform is named, was driven by his non-conformist Christian beliefs. In 1773, he was appointed High Sheriff for Bedfordshire and embarked upon an inspection and exposé of prison conditions that became his life's work. He published detailed statistics to substantiate his findings, making him one of the first to appreciate the value of monitoring and evaluation! He also pressed for a chaplaincy service in prisons, believing that spiritual starvation was a major obstacle to reformation of character.

Justices of the Peace were authorized, by Act of Parliament, to appoint salaried chaplains to local prisons in England and Wales from 1773. However, it was not an easy task, as William Noblett, current Chaplain General, explains:

> The first chaplains attended to the sick and those about to be executed, but some found their task depressing and unrewarding. Complaints arose that such men could not do much in a prison which echoed with profaneness and blasphemy. The same might be thought true today! But ministry is partly about faithfulness, and the continuous and renewed call to be where God's people are, in whatever circumstances.[2]

In the design for a new breed of Victorian prisons – many of which remain in use today – the chapel was placed at the very heart of the building, and every warder carried a Bible. This reflected the, by now, popular view that evangelism was the answer to crime. But, as William Noblett records, the experiment was not a success: 'it proved that even the coercion of the penitentiary cannot bring about change, without a heart which is open to the love of God'.[3]

Resettlement of those released from custody was first seen as an important issue towards the end of the nineteenth century, and it was the Church that provided the first 'Police Court Missionaries' to rescue some of those who had come before the courts. In 1876 a Hertfordshire printer, Frederick Rainer, wrote to the Church of England Temperance Society, deploring the fact that 'once a person was convicted and imprisoned there seemed no hope for him, only "offence after offence, sentence after sentence"'.[4]

Rainer sent five shillings to help start some practical work with drunks to break this vicious circle. By 1900 the Police Court Mission employed more than a hundred people in London and elsewhere, forerunners of today's probation officers. One of the early missionaries wrote:

> I saw men shorn of all glory. I saw womanhood clothed in shame.
> I saw vice rampant. I saw women with bruised and battered faces.
> I saw children old before their time. I saw young men to whom
> obscenity was the very breath of life. I saw young women, half
> beast, half human.[5]

The Probation of Offenders Act in 1907 launched the modern probation service, and the Criminal Justice Act of 1948 set out that probation officers should supervise offenders and 'advise, assist and befriend them'. Today, the focus of probation work is more on public protection, risk management and behaviour change; it is once again faith-based and other voluntary sector groups are helping to fill the role of advising, assisting and befriending offenders post-release.

The range of these organizations is impressive and it is appropriate that their role should be affirmed and celebrated in this report. I have begun with examples of projects that have a national profile; all use volunteers. There are many more; inclusion is not meant to imply that those mentioned are of greater worth than others that are not. (Contact and web site details are included in the Notes section.)

During the past two years, more than 400 discharged prisoners have been linked with church congregations through the resettlement work of Alpha for Prisons. At least 60 per cent of those have settled sufficiently to avoid further conviction and re-imprisonment. Although Alpha for Prisons began as an evangelical outreach, and Alpha courses have been run for 30,000 men and women in prison, resettlement now represents a larger part of the work. Alpha produces a training manual and recommends that churches have an agreement, or contract, with released prisoners, setting out expectations and ground rules. It is hoping to develop a network of local advisors who will help when difficulties arise.[6]

The Mothers' Union is a worldwide Anglican organization promoting the well-being of families through practical projects established by volunteers within local communities. Members seek to offer that same support and encouragement to those separated from their families by imprisonment.

Over 1,000 volunteers are active in 80 prisons, in befriending schemes, women's support groups, work with children in visits halls and visitor centres, chaplaincy teams, and facilitating parenting groups or courses. Though the work undertaken by MU volunteers is varied, the needs to which they are seeking to respond are consistently similar: isolation, loneliness and a sense of grief, caused by separation from family and friends. Guidelines for MU members working in prisons are provided and can be accessed via the web site – look for the members' section and then click on UK project guidelines.[7]

Pacer 50plus is a national support network for older serving and former prisoners. As a former prisoner, the founder, Stuart Ware, found that the pains of imprisonment continue long after release. In fact, he says the negative experiences of imprisonment have become a major contributor to recidivism; overcrowded prisons are becoming places for human warehousing and containment, where the emphasis is on risk assessment rather than rehabilitation. Our criminal justice and penal systems are failing to reintegrate offenders in their local communities once they have completed their punishment. Yet, healing and reconciliation are a central feature of the Christian gospel. Stuart Ware says he is fortunate in that he has faith, which has been informed by experiences that compel him to minister to the needs of older prisoners, some of whom will die in prison. Reconciliation lies at the heart of the work of Pacer 50plus.[8]

Care Remand Fostering is a Christian project specializing in providing accommodation for young offenders who would otherwise be remanded to custody. The work was started in Reading and there are now centres in Chelmsford and Stockton-on-Tees, with a fourth opening in Birmingham. The service is designed to be user friendly for youth offending teams, with a telephone referral system, transport to court and same day placements. A foster home (only one young offender at a time) and an activities programme to meet the young person's individual needs are provided. All young people are moved away from their home area so that they can benefit from a new start and clear boundaries. Results so far are very encouraging; most of the young people complete the programme and go on to receive a community sentence.[9]

Depaul Trust was founded as a Catholic response to the growing number of young homeless people arriving in London. It has developed a range of services including night shelters, hostels, employment training and family mediation. In 1998, Depaul Trust began working with young offenders through two projects, Outside Link and One-to-One. The Outside Link helps young prison leavers secure accommodation before release, in order to prevent them from being homeless and vulnerable to reoffending. The One-to-One project matches young offenders about to be released with volunteers who provide support and advice to help them live independently and be integrated into the community. Both projects have demonstrated a reduced rate of re-offending.[10]

The Prison Advice and Care Trust (PACT) came into being in 2001 as the result of a merger of The Bourne Trust and Prisoners' Wives and Families Society (PWFS). The Bourne Trust was founded by two Catholic lawyers to provide better services for prisoners and prisoners' families; their motive for action was their Christian faith. PWFS was founded when a group of prisoners' wives met together to discuss their problems and to support one another. Their motive for action was one of self-help. PACT works with prisoners who have mental health needs, both male and female, and supports prisoners' families, working towards successful integration of ex-offenders back into the community. PACT provides a free national telephone helpline, visitor centre management in prisons in the Greater London area and the south-west of England, supervised play for children visiting prison, all-day children's visits, counselling for remand prisoners, and a first night in custody service in HMP Holloway for women with mental health needs.[11]

Prison Fellowship is motivated by Christ's words: 'I was in prison and you visited me' (Matthew 25.36). Volunteers and staff from all Christian denominations show the love of Christ to prisoners, prisoners' families and ex-offenders, regardless of their beliefs. Working with prison chaplains, volunteers based in more than 150 local groups of Prison Fellowship England and Wales provide ongoing support to prisoners. Many befriend prisoners' families and ex-offenders. Special projects are run by trained volunteers and staff. Based on the Bible story of Zacchaeus' encounter with Christ, Sycamore Tree is a programme for prisoners on victim awareness and restorative justice. Prisoners hear from volunteers who have been victims of crime and take part in symbolic acts of restitution. Through the Angel Tree project, local groups raise funds to buy, wrap and deliver Christmas presents for prisoners' children. It is an excellent way of strengthening family ties. The Compass project, based at Highpoint Prison in Suffolk is a six-month Christian values-based programme for prisoners that covers life skills, Christian lifestyle and the arts.[12]

Some of the most innovative projects are local, perhaps started by an individual or a small group who saw a need for, or had a vision of, what might be achieved, and refused to be deterred by setbacks. The Churches' Criminal Justice Forum (CCJF) seeks to publicize such projects, so that

Christians in other areas might be challenged to think about whether they could try something similar. Again, these are only examples; one of the most exciting aspects of the work of CCJF is the constant discovery of new ventures, started by imaginative, energetic and faithful people.

No one who has met the team of six prisoners who work as trained advisers at the Oxford Citizens Advice Bureau can fail to be impressed by their commitment, and their learning from the experience and the responsibility they are given. They have been warmly received by others at the Bureau, who respect them for their professionalism and the major contribution they have made to meeting client needs. Partly as a result of having these new advisers from the Springhill Prison partnership, the Bureau has been able to answer nine out of ten telephone enquiries, where previously it could answer only one in twenty.

While working in the chaplaincy at Low Newton women's prison at Durham, Elizabeth McGurk became aware that many women had no one to meet them on discharge, and were apprehensive about getting themselves to the railway or bus station. A plan was drawn up to have a team of volunteer drivers available. Elizabeth spoke about this at three Sunday Masses in her own church, St Joseph's, Gilesgate; she expected maybe six to volunteer, and when forty came forward she says 'I knew this was a work of the Holy Spirit'. There have been obstacles to overcome, but the scheme is now working well. Some women have been taken directly to their probation office and hostel, ensuring that they keep appointments, which, if missed, could mean immediate return to prison.

The Surrey Appropriate Adult Volunteer Scheme supports vulnerable detainees in police custody. Sixty trained volunteers try to ensure that the person's rights are observed and that they understand why they have been arrested. They also support detainees through the custody process, including the interview, and they encourage detainees to consider taking legal advice (but do not themselves give such advice). The service operates 24 hours a day for 365 days a year and has successfully responded to more than 9,000 calls since 1995. Staff at custody centres in Staines, Reigate, Woking and Guildford are supplied with the names of volunteers and call them in turn. The scheme supports young people aged 16 and under, where parents or guardians are not available, and adults who are judged to be vulnerable, mainly through mental illness or learning disability. The scheme is a partnership project of the Diocese of Guildford Department of Social Responsibility. The staff and many volunteers are inspired by their faith to be involved in delivering a fair and non-discriminatory justice process. Funding is provided by Surrey County

Council Adult Services and Surrey Youth Offending Team with support from the Diocese of Guildford Board of Finance.[13]

Revive Enterprise in south-east Northumberland seeks to support disadvantaged people through Christian social action, and to give experience of work to people aged 16 to 25, who are long-term unemployed and may have been in trouble with the law. Revive collects donated furniture and makes it available to those in need. Trainees work alongside project staff in planning collection and delivery routes, assessing stock and demand levels, and developing warehouse management and customer service skills.[14]

The Amelia Methodist Trust farm near Cardiff works with disaffected young people. Many come from dysfunctional families, have been excluded from mainstream schooling, and get caught up in the criminal justice system. Outdoor, environmental and workshop activities operate alongside basic literacy and numeracy teaching. Some young people obtain qualifications, others simply leave with increased confidence and self-esteem and are better able to cope. Volunteers are an essential part of the workforce; many of the young people who have left come back to help. Underpinning everything is a strong belief that a sense of God is frequently found in creation, beauty, the countryside and relationships. For many young people, the farm is a special place, and a sanctuary.[15]

While many resources are channelled into responding to offending, Oxford Youth Works tries to prevent it. The project builds relationships with young people as an expression of Christian care that tries to reflect the motivation and method of Jesus. It tends to be the more needy and at-risk young people who respond, although they are not specifically targeted. The security that can be provided by this relationship means that young people are more open to challenge and change. Oxford Youth Works focuses on relationships with and between young people and their communities and encourages restorative approaches to all levels of conflict. One initiative in particular is working to transform deep-rooted destructive behaviour patterns and help young people develop their ability to repair damaged relationships.[16]

Kainos Community (KC) runs rehabilitative/therapeutic programmes at the Verne prison in Dorset and at Swaleside prison on the Isle of Sheppey. Prisoners volunteer to join these programmes and are expected to stay for a minimum of six months. The basic ethos of KC is that prisoners develop life skills through 24-hour community living, learning respect both for themselves and others. They gain insight into the way they think, and so are better able to understand their own behaviour and are helped to change. It is a learning experience in which peers and staff give prisoners feedback and support. Although the programme is based on Christian values, it is not a religious programme. Prisoners of all faiths or no faith are welcome. Volunteers are an important part of the programme; they range from 25 to more than 80 years of age. There are considerable benefits to the establishments in which KC operates, by improvement in the behaviour of the prisoners. There is also growing evidence that men who have completed the programme are less likely to reoffend.[17]

Stepping Stones is a Christian Trust that has been working with ex-offenders for 20 years, helping them move forward into decent homes and worthwhile jobs, with a supporting church. The Trust has three houses in London for those guilty of mainstream offences, and for those who have committed sex offences. St Mark's Church, Battersea Rise and the New Life Christian Centre in Croydon strengthen and encourage the men, and provide them with voluntary jobs. There are daily devotions in each house, as well as individual mentoring and help with improving life skills. In addition, each resident is given help with suitable training and, if required, Christian counselling, for his life in the future.[18]

People of faith also bring energy, commitment and vision to many secular roles within criminal justice.

Official Prison Visitors visit men, women and young offenders in almost all prison establishments throughout England and Wales. Prisoners ask to have a Prison Visitor to talk to on a regular and confidential basis. Visitors give those they visit a sense of self-worth and dignity, helping them to discover new ways of living. The National Association of Official Prison Visitors is not a religious organization although many are motivated by a personal faith. Visitors come from all walks of life and commit to visit, on a regular basis, any prisoner who asks, regardless of creed, race or crime.[19]

Prisoners' Penfriends enables people who care about prisoners to make friendships through the post. It provides a secure forwarding service to ensure that addresses (and, if required, names) are not revealed to prisoners. There are guidelines for correspondents to make sure that appropriate security measures are followed, and there is an advice service should any problems arise. When funds permit, there will be a newsletter for all correspondents to share news and ideas. Prisoners' Penfriends is not a specifically Christian organization (and is emphatically not in existence to attempt to convert prisoners to any religious viewpoint), but those members who are Christians will remember that Jesus has told us that, when we help a prisoner, we are helping him.[20]

Inside Out Trust works in more than 80 prisons. Restorative projects involve prisoners in work that helps them to develop new skills and – most importantly – to improve the lives of other people. These include large-scale park regeneration schemes, Braille transcription for blind children and adults, art for hospices and wheelchairs for disabled people in Africa. Prisoners volunteer for this work, and it is important that they do so. Helping other people must be a deliberate act! Volunteers from outside support the prisoner project teams in a variety of ways: encouraging, training, praising and awarding certificates. Although the Inside Out Trust is not a Christian-based organization, many of the staff and volunteers have a faith background, which they bring to their work. The team believes strongly that each individual needs self-respect and a positive sense of having a place in the world in order to thrive, and that this must include the most vulnerable people in our society, particularly people in prison.[21]

Parents in Prison (PIP) offers mothers and fathers in prison the opportunity to record a bedtime story for their child, and add a personal message. Tapes are sent all over the world, with PIP covering the costs. Most PIP volunteers are drawn from churches. At present, there are projects at Leeds, Highpoint in Suffolk, Holloway and Wandsworth in London and Eastwood Park near Bristol. PIP would love to hear from new volunteers, or any church group that would like to support its work.[22]

In 2004, the National Association of Victims Support Schemes marks 30 years of support to victims of crime and witnesses in court, with its fundamental principle of the restorative value of a community response to those attacked in their community. Its diverse resource of 12,000 volunteers provides practical help and emotional support for those whose lives are turned upside down as a victim, or witness, of crime. Victim Support finds that its help is often sought by relatives and friends of those directly affected by the crime, for the impact of a burglary, serious sexual assault or bullying is rarely limited to the individual. Assistance with criminal injuries claims and attending court to give evidence, and having their story and its consequences heard, perhaps repeatedly, are the day-to-day services freely given by volunteers, trained and supported by professional staff.[23]

Local lay magistrates dispense justice in 96 per cent of all criminal cases. Few people realize that almost anyone can apply to become a magistrate, and, recently, the age for application has been lowered from 27 to 18. The Lord Chancellor, responsible for recruiting and appointing magistrates through local advisory committees, requires magistrates to have six key qualities: good character, understanding and communication, social awareness, maturity and sound temperament, sound judgement, and commitment and reliability. Magistrates take very serious decisions that can impact heavily on someone's life and, consequently, the lives of other family members. As far as possible, the group of magistrates assigned to a court, who sit as a bench of three, reflects the community in which the court sits and there should be a mix of gender, ethnic minority, marital status, sexual orientation, religion, occupation and employment. Being a magistrate is a serious commitment but one that brings a great deal of responsibility, humility and fulfilment.[24]

There are also, of course, many Christian police, prison and probation officers, social workers and members of youth offending teams who see their work, not as being evangelical, but as a practical expression of their faith (James 2.14-26).

Those who do develop an interest can find that it becomes a passion, as it did for Elizabeth Fry and John Howard. I went to speak at a church one Sunday morning on behalf of the Churches' Criminal Justice Forum, and was asked if I had been invited by 'Grace'. I did not know to whom the questioner referred. After the service, another worshipper asked if I was a friend of 'Grace'. Over tea, I met this frail, silver-haired woman who had helped to run a befriending group at a women's prison. It was clear that everyone at that church had been encouraged to share the sorrows and joys of those she visited. I left with the thought that every church needed Grace. The 'Grace' at this church had come to know not a system, not cases, but real people, in need of healing and restoration.

When I first became a volunteer Prison Visitor, many years ago, my own mother was less than enthusiastic. 'Why waste time on them?' she asked. I told her about the man I was visiting. He was in his late sixties, had been in prison for 20 years and had no surviving family. His sight was poor and, like so many offenders, he could barely read and write. A week later, my mother produced a book she had bought with large coloured pictures, and asked if it would be in order for me to take this when next I visited. The offence committed was horrible, but the plight of the sinner had transcended the sin.

Churches not only demonstrate compassion, through Churches' Criminal Justice Forum they continue to highlight the shortcomings of the system, and to call for reform. In 1999, the Church of England produced a report on the rehabilitation of sex offenders in congregations, which sold 6,000 copies.[25] It also engaged the new Labour Government in discussion about criminal justice policy and worked with Inquest and Churches' Commission for Racial Justice to highlight concerns about deaths in police custody.

Also in 1999, the Catholic Agency for Social Concern (now Caritas – social action) produced, for the Catholic Bishops' Conference of England and Wales, a report drawing attention to the particular negative consequences of the increasingly common practice of imprisoning women.[26] It argued that this was likely to have little positive impact on crime levels, but did have negative consequences for families. It suggested that all possible steps should be taken to strengthen the possibility of maintaining ties between women in prison and their children and that positive alternatives to prison should be encouraged. When it was published, *Women in Prison* had the backing of the (then) Church of England Board for Social Responsibility; the United Reformed Church, Church and Society Committee; the Methodist Church; the Baptist Union of Great Britain, Department of Research and Training in Mission; the Britain Yearly Meeting of the Religious Society of Friends (Quakers), Crime and Justice Committee; and the General Assembly of Unitarian and Free Christian Churches, Penal Affairs Panel.

It was quickly realized that churches acting together, in an area that did not, for the most part, present obstacles of differing theological understanding, had a much stronger voice than churches acting separately. An ecumenical working group was established as a forum through which the churches could together seek to progress the report's recommendations. This was joined by representatives of those denominations who had supported the original report, plus both the Salvation Army and the New Testament Church of God. In 2001, the name Churches' Criminal Justice Forum was adopted to reflect the group's interest in a range of criminal justice issues, and CCJF was accepted as a Network of Churches Together in Britain and Ireland.

The purpose of CCJF is to uphold Christian values in the field of criminal justice. It seeks to raise awareness of criminal justice concerns in local churches, to stress the relevance of criminal justice to Christian teaching, and it encourages churchgoing people to get involved in the ways already detailed.

CCJF promotes the development of restorative justice (described in Tim Newell's contribution) as being an approach that embraces many principles of Christian teaching such as right behaviour (John 8.11), repentance (Luke 23.39-44), forgiveness (Matthew 6.14-15), healing (Isaiah 61.1-2) and restoration (Luke 15.11-24). Most of all, it recognizes the value of each and every individual, be that person victim or offender. As Christians, we believe that we are all made in God's image and are therefore precious to him, and that we are all 'offenders' before him, yet are still loved by him (Romans 3.22-24). We share a belief that we are all capable of change.

Two Salvation Army officers are seconded to CCJF, to assist in the development of local community chaplaincy projects in which volunteers are recruited from churches and other faith communities to work under the direction of a coordinator, or community chaplain, in advising, befriending and mentoring people released from prison, particularly those serving short sentences, who are less likely to receive assistance from statutory services such as probation. At the time of writing, schemes are operating in Swansea, Preston and Gloucester and are beginning to demonstrate that people who receive this kind of assistance are less likely to reoffend. CCJF has also helped establish a dialogue on shared criminal justice concerns with other faiths, and at least one community chaplaincy scheme currently in the course of development – in Leeds – is a multi-faith initiative.

CCJF is in discussion with politicians, particularly to urge policies that address aspects of social exclusion that are major factors in offending.[27] The Social Exclusion Unit has identified that issues such as lack of supportive family, failure to engage with education, lack of life skills, unemployment and homelessness are all significant factors in offending.[28] These are practical challenges that many of the faith-based projects address. Largely because it represents the churches acting together, CCJF has been able to meet with successive Prisons and Probation Ministers (Paul Boateng, Hilary Benn and Paul Goggins) as well as with Dominic Grieve, Conservative criminal justice spokesman, and Simon Hughes, former Liberal Democrat Home Affairs spokesman. Dominic Grieve and Paul Goggins both spoke at CCJF Network meetings in 2003 and Simon Hughes launched *What Can I Do?*, a booklet suggesting how people can get usefully involved in the criminal justice system. This is produced jointly by CCJF and the Prison Advice and Care Trust and funded by the Rethinking Crime and Punishment project of the Esmée Fairbairn Foundation.[29]

Through fortunate, (or God-inspired?) timing, CCJF was being launched just as the three-year Rethinking Crime and Punishment initiative was beginning a comprehensive grant-making programme, and CCJF was able to obtain funding to appoint, full-time for two years, a Criminal Justice, or Education Officer, effectively to do in the churches, from a Christian standpoint, what RCP sought to do in the nation: to encourage people to rethink their approach to crime and punishment. I took up that post in March 2002, after 15 years as a probation officer.

With this staff resource, CCJF has been able to:

- launch a web site[30] and a quarterly newsletter that now goes to 650 organizations and individuals, including church leaders;
- host meetings twice a year, to give those on the mailing list the opportunity to hear from prominent speakers and to exchange news about local initiatives;
- respond to invitations to speak and discuss issues with local churches;
- write articles for many Christian and secular publications;
- promote the *What Can I Do?* booklet;
- share criminal justice concerns at Spring Harvest, Greenbelt and Alpha for Prisons 'Caring for Ex-Offenders' training days;
- mount regional awareness-raising events in Cardiff, in collaboration with The Society for Promoting Christian Knowledge;
- promote best practice in family visiting facilities in women's prisons in north-east England, in collaboration with NEPACS (formerly the North Eastern After Care Society), which helps with Prison Visitor centres, play areas, and visits for children and teenagers.

With funding secured to employ the Criminal Justice Officer for a further two years, CCJF wants, additionally, to:

- produce a course of home study material on Christianity and criminal justice to offer to local churches;
- encourage the establishment of local Christian criminal justice forums, which will form a bridge between CCJF nationally and local churches;
- establish a dialogue with black-majority churches to discuss and pursue appropriate responses to the over-representation of black people among the prison population. (It was recently calculated that, if white people were imprisoned at the same rate as black people, there would be not seventy-four thousand, but half a million, people in the already overcrowded prisons of England and Wales.)

The challenge remains to convince people, and particularly church-going people – who may never have come into contact with criminal justice – that it is something they *should* be concerned about. I recently received letters from a couple whose son, aged 18 and without previous convictions, received a three-and-a-half-year sentence in a Young Offender Institution. They knew nothing of how the system works; now, they say their 'eyes have been opened to the horrors of prison life'. They write:

> The media consistently presents an image of prison and sentencing that is very far from the truth. It is quite likely, because of this misrepresentation, that tougher sentences are now becoming the norm . . . Prisons bear no resemblance to holiday camps . . . Why

is prison seen as a solution to crime when it is anything but? . . .
Prison really should be the very last resort. There is nothing
positive about imprisonment; it robs people of their humanity,
their dignity . . . The powers-that-be still cannot see that this
environment will almost guarantee reoffending.

The purpose of quoting from their letter is not merely to highlight the
limitations of prison in reducing offending; that is only a small part of the
brief of CCJF. It is to highlight the ignorance there is among those who
have never brushed with the system. It is a policy issue, but it is also a
human issue. CCJF invites those with whom it engages to consider that
criminal justice is not only about broken laws, it is also about broken lives
– the lives of victims, the lives of offenders, and of communities. Jesus
was especially good with those whose lives were broken, and he
commended his approach to us.

chapter 5

the future of sentencing: a perspective from the judiciary

Lord Justice Laws

I am not sure that I have much to say about the *future* of sentencing, since that must lie to a considerable extent in the hands of our legislators; and it would not be apt for me as a serving judge to prognosticate about what the legislators might do, even if I could claim (which I cannot) any special perception in the matter. I can only say a little about the *nature* of sentencing, which might perhaps be relevant to others' consideration of questions about the future.

It is trite that the focus of a criminal judge is upon the justice of the particular case before him or her. And I think many judges would agree that the cases in which it is most difficult to achieve justice – or, at least, justice as one sees it – are not the headline crimes. Convictions for very serious offences such as rape, armed robbery, wounding with intent and so on are bound, save in very exceptional circumstances, to attract prison sentences, and the only question for the judge is how long the prison sentence should be. That is, of course, a question of great importance for the offender, and indeed for the victim. But it is by no means as difficult for the judge as it is to decide in a marginal case – perhaps burglary of a shop when no one was there to be frightened – whether to send the offender to prison at all, or whether a community penalty would suffice.

Murder cases are in a way the easiest of all to sentence. Statute prescribes only one lawful punishment, imprisonment for life; so the judge has no choice. There can, of course, be acute difficulties in the decision how long the offender should actually serve to satisfy the requirements of retributive justice. The compulsory sentence of life imprisonment is an anomaly that owes its origins, I understand, to a political deal done when the death penalty was abolished in 1965. If our criminal law is reformed so as to abolish the crimes of murder and manslaughter and substitute them with a single offence of unlawful killing for which the sentence will depend on the gravity of the individual case, the anomaly will be removed.

The judge's day-to-day workload, then, involves acute concentration on the individual facts of one case after another. He or she does not, of course, carry out this task in a vacuum. For many types of offence, there are guideline decisions of the Court of Appeal Criminal Division. For others, there will be cases in the books that may help the judge, even if there are no guidelines. For all crimes created by statute (and that is nearly all that there are) Parliament has set a maximum penalty. But, within this sentencing architecture (to use far too grand a phrase), the judge still has to decide the individual case, and he or she will concentrate on its individual facts.

So much is perhaps all too obvious. But there are features of the sentencing judge's ordinary work that suggest, at least to my mind, some deeper issues to be considered. I would mention two in particular. Firstly, the necessarily pragmatic approach of sitting judges does not encourage them to think about *theories* of punishment. They are not philosophers, neither do I suggest that they become philosophers. But the work's intense concentration on the individual case has perhaps meant that, when the courts are actually required to think about the purpose, nature and justification of punishment at a more general level, as sometimes they can be, the result is sometimes superficial.

Secondly, the space given within the architecture for judges to make up their minds across a range of sentences that might be imposed in the particular case is a measure of the extent to which the law regards sentencing as a judicial and not a political process. Murder is the only offence for which there is a single available penalty prescribed by Parliament. There are other recent instances in which the Government has obtained legislation to fix *minimum* sentences in certain cases. Where the judges have seemed to be, or have been reported to be, reluctant to apply such measures wholeheartedly but have sought to find a wider discretionary power in let-out provisions referring to exceptional or special circumstances, that has not been the result of any instinct to be tender towards the criminal. It has arisen out of a concern that the more the judges' sentencing hands are tied by Parliament, the more the sentencing exercise is actually in the hands of the political arm of the State: and that is a troublesome development.

Let me return to our relative unconcern with punishment theory. I have said that some of our perceptions in this area have been superficial. Thus we have not been at pains to distinguish between the idea of retribution and the idea of deterrence, yet they are entirely different things. Deterrence has nothing to do with distributive or proportionate justice. If there were a law prescribing a mandatory death sentence for any driver caught going through a red traffic light, you can be sure that no one, or at least no one sane and sober, would commit the offence. The example is, of course, fanciful, but what it shows is that a punitive measure might have an extremely satisfactory deterrent effect if it were not constrained by the principle of retribution. Yet retribution and deterrence in various sentencing contexts are lumped together, although, in fact, there is a necessary and desirable tension between them.

I should explain what I mean by the principle of retribution. Its confusion with the idea of revenge is an old chestnut. Retribution, unlike revenge, is a civilizing principle, because it involves moderation and proportionality. Now, it is obviously open to argument how severely crimes like rape or robbery should be dealt with. One thing the principle of retribution tells us is that they should be dealt with a great deal more severely than those of shoplifting or driving through red traffic lights. It means there must be a rational structure in a punishment system so that penalties imposed reflect the gravity of the crime. It means, in particular, that an offender should be punished *no more severely* than he or she deserves within the principles involved in that structure.

The retributive principle is thus very important, and it is to be sharply distinguished from revenge. This has nothing to do with justice, only with the victim's desire to inflict the same suffering as she or he has suffered. If the legal system were to allow the victim to choose the defendant's penalty, it would be a system driven by hatred. It is vital that the difference between such a barbarism and the proper application of the principle of retribution should be understood and recognized. Newspapers that bray for a criminal's blood do as great a disservice to the public good in this context as do the woolliest of liberals.

There is here a very hard lesson to be learned. The agonized spouse, parent or child who has lost a loved one through a repellent and violent crime and calls for the perpetrator to be locked up and the key thrown away – or more – is not calling for justice, however great the sympathy evoked. He or she is calling for revenge. Revenge has nothing whatever do with justice. And it has nothing whatever to do with retribution.

There are two more things to say. Firstly, despite the importance of the retributive principle as a brake on excessive punishments, in some cases the courts advisedly depart from it. Thus, for instance, where an armed robber is held by the trial judge, on objective evidence, to represent an unpredictable danger into the future, the court may impose a sentence of life imprisonment. This is avowedly done *not* on the footing that the criminal deserves to be locked up for life as a matter of retributive justice. In such a case the court is required to state the finite term of years to be served in order to satisfy the retributive principle. The life sentence is imposed so that the criminal may be detained for *longer* than he or she deserves, at the discretion of the Home Office, for the protection of the public. And there are certain other circumstances in which an extended sentence may be ordered. I think it important to recognize that, when the court passes such sentences, it is not performing its paradigm function in sentencing, which is the execution of retributive justice. It is performing a social service, given to it by statute, of public protection. The moral justification of such orders is akin to the justification of an order made under the Mental Health Act for the compulsory admission to hospital of a person whose condition poses a threat to him- or herself or others.

Secondly, the subtle amalgam of retribution and other interests, which is characteristic of a developed sentencing system such as ours, can only operate successfully in a culture of legislative restraint. It is not just a matter of territory: the judges' and the politicians' territory. At least as important is this: the closer Parliament comes to legislating for specific cases, the closer we are to rule-book justice. Rule-book justice is barbarous. It treats the criminal not as an individual, but merely as a member of a class, to be dealt with according to the rules set to govern the class. If the State systematically looks at its citizens, even the most flawed among them, in that grim light, it looks at them as things not people.

restorative justice in a money culture: overcoming the obstacles to a restorative rationality

Peter Selby

The case for making restoration the primary objective of a criminal justice system is so obvious that it is perhaps important to include in this collection some suggestions about the obstacles that prevent people from accepting it, and how they can be overcome. Even such moving, and widely publicized, approaches to criminal acts as the Truth and Reconciliation process in South Africa are often described as 'idealistic' (in a clearly pejorative sense). That is, they are thought to belong to a world that is in principle unrealizable. The real or imagined failures of such processes are often recounted, it would appear, for the purpose of providing comfort to those who would wish to remain clear that 'in the real world' such an approach will never work.

Thus the 'real world' of crime figures – no-go estates, antisocial behaviour, overstretched police forces and an electorate ever more stirred up to punitive attitudes by a press always able to sell papers by outpourings of outrage at the latest high-profile crime – are ranged against 'idealism' and 'pure theory' (religious faith belonging clearly to that department of life) and declared too weak to survive. It seems not enough to show that:

> [c]learly the Restorative Justice approach provides a much more satisfying answer to the traditional philosophical and jurisprudential questions of criminal justice than any other of the major theories . . . It provides a far more convincing account of how punishment can 'make things right' than does the retributive theory. It addresses the question of social protection and deterrence, which is the primary concern of the utilitarian theory. It has a far more morally acceptable view of rehabilitation than does the traditional therapeutically oriented rehabilitation theory. It has a socially much richer view of what is involved in compensation for victims of punishment than does the libertarian restitutionist view.[1]

These theoretical advantages, even backed also by the record of religious
wisdom of ancient cultures and the experience of mediation, conciliation
and other 'restorative' processes, somehow fail to convert the heart and
convince the mind (both seem to be required; both seem to be difficult)
of those with responsibility for penal policy that restorative justice could
'work', or be presented to the public in such a way as to gain electoral
support. It does not even seem to be sufficient to recount examples within
our present prison and probation systems, or offered by voluntary groups,
that show that the lives of convicted people can be changed for the better
and victims of crime enabled to move on from their experience. It seems
to remain exceptionally easy to present restorative processes as 'soft',
created in the interests of criminals and against the interests of victims,
by people who do not live in areas of high criminality or inhabit 'the
real world'.

the punitive context

The famous statement of the Home Secretary that he wanted judges
who inhabited the same real world as he did[2] invites some reflection on
the character of that 'real world', which in his mind should, and in this
writer's mind does, constitute the context in which current sentencing
policy is worked out. For this is not at its heart a question about the
wisdom, compassion or firmness of this or that magistrate or judge.
Rather it is a matter of a powerful background culture or ethos, a
conditioning that affects the thinking of all involved in the penal system
without declaring itself or being openly recognized. Deeply-rooted
principles, disputed by almost nobody as long as they remain principles
only, such as 'the independence of the judiciary' can easily mask such
a pervasive influence, one that makes it hard for any of us to defend
our 'independence' of thought and action, however strong our convictions
and firm our intellectual grasp of the pressures being brought to bear on
us by our context.

On the surface, the context in which we are operating in matters to do
with crime is indeed punitive, and increasingly so. The language of the
political debate about crime, let alone the style of the reporting in the
newspapers with the largest readership, leaves one in no doubt that
punishment, in the sense of retribution that fits the crime, is the most
widely accepted strategy for dealing with those who break the law or
behave in antisocial ways. A current example of this is in some immediate
responses to the campaign to restore to convicted prisoners the right to
vote: 'They have demonstrated that they don't deserve the vote' is a

statement that conveniently ignores the point that voting is not a privilege anyone else has to 'deserve'.

What is more significant in relation to a commendation of a restorative justice is that the punitive rhetoric is nearly always combined with the rhetoric of concern for the *victims* of crime. It is the repeated, though unexamined, assumption of those who advocate firm retribution that the ferocity of the sentences they demand is a demonstration of their support for the victim and, conversely, that those who support prison reform and an emphasis on rehabilitation are demonstrating a lack of regard for those who suffer the effects of crime and a preferential option for those who commit it.

One analysis of this rhetoric would involve looking at the sheer violence of it. A senior police officer in our area once pointed out to our staff meeting the importance of removing violent language from the work of reducing criminal activity: if we speak of a police *force* and of the importance of *fighting* crime we should expect that one effect of our language will be generally to increase the context of violence by which society is pervaded. Indeed, to read much of the rhetoric of the battle against crime is to experience a great uncertainty whether it is with the criminal or society at large that the origins of violent crime are to be found.

Another feature of this violent rhetoric, however, is its total failure to examine what kind of response to crime would, in fact, benefit the victim. To experience rage or outrage (the two are not always to be distinguished) on reading of a violent crime against a defenceless person is entirely human, and is what is to be expected from a sentient, and in particular a *morally* sentient, being; to expect that reaction to be acted out by society at large, embodied in statute and in the institutions of the criminal justice system, is quite another matter. For to ask for that is to make the judgement that such a passionate response is to be nourished, perhaps massaged, as though the sensation of having such responses acted out is the most therapeutic option *for the victim and his or her supporters*. Yet, at another time, the same person will acknowledge, in the words of the cliché, that there's no point bearing grudges. The acting out of retributive desires does little to benefit the person who has them, as the lined faces of embittered victims all too often testify. It is well understood – when we are not thinking about criminality – that there is no requiting of the longing for revenge, and certainly that the carrying out of revenge does not quieten the angry heart. The essential *mutuality* of the benefits of forgiveness is one of the aspects of Christ's teaching on this subject that can most readily be commended to all, believers or not, on the basis of our common human experience.

the financial metaphor

However, the language of violence is not the only one deployed in the rhetoric of popular, and populist, responses to crime. At least as prevalent, and probably more revealing of the context within which the debate on the criminal justice system and its aims is conducted, is the language of economics and finance. If there is so much as a grain of truth in Nietzsche's comment that morality began when the first buyer met the first seller, it is certainly the case that criminality began at that point, and continues to be supported and discussed in the language of commerce. The language of the repaying of a convicted person's 'debt to society' is as revealing of what are thought to be the aims of the criminal justice system as it is irrational. For the fact is that, if we are to speak of serious crimes as 'debts', then those debts have to be placed in the category of debts that are in principle unrepayable. Whatever would discharge the obligation to a victim of serious crime, it cannot, surely, be some act of suffering on the part of the criminal. What kind of 'payment' either to victim or to the wider society would actually 'compensate' for the suffering of a murder or a rape? The purpose of noticing the intrusion of financial language, and especially the language of indebtedness, is not to honour it as offering a rational account but to take seriously the power of the financial/economic nexus of thinking to condition responses in areas of life to which it has in truth no relevance.

The use of the language of 'tariff' is particularly instructive in this regard. In speaking of a judge, or the Home Secretary, setting a 'tariff' for a particular crime, the intention is that, *before* consideration of the progress of the offender, their behaviour in prison or the level of danger they pose to society at large, there should be established what the level of punishment *deserved* is for the crime in question. Issues of remorse, reform or deterrence are precisely what may *not* carry weight in the determination of the tariff; the only consideration is the *seriousness* of the crime and, therefore, the level of *payment* required to satisfy the *debt* incurred to society by the criminal.

The financial language in the rhetoric of crime and punishment has, of course, the special attraction of the appearance of objectivity. 'Seriousness' is measured in terms of months or years in prison, so that with 'tariffs' go, of necessity, 'differentials'. 'Incentives' and 'discounts', 'remissions' and 'rewards' will also feature prominently in a landscape of punishment in which financial metaphors predominate. The public becomes well accustomed to headlines and newspaper articles that draw attention to the failure of some judge to exact the penalty that is proportionate to the seriousness of an offence, one who has, so to speak, got the numbers wrong.

In the more minor areas of criminality – as motoring offences are reckoned to be – the 'tariff' system offers swift justice, with actual tariffs – in money – related to particular degrees of excess speed, and the number of points on a licence similarly listed against particular offences. The value of such a system in dispensing swift and predictable penalties has to be weighed against the reality that, for those who can afford to see them in this way, the difference between a 'fine' – which is punishment – and a 'charge' – which is levied as the price of a particular activity, as in the London 'congestion charge' – is elided. People who place a value on their time can well decide, factoring the risk of detection into their calculation, that parking on a double yellow line is 'worth it', and speeding can be also. A person who does this may well be surprised, and even morally affronted, that the burglar or fraudster carries out a similar calculation. The proposal in some police areas to offer the driver caught speeding the alternative of paying for a 'speed awareness' course suggests that, even for motorists, restorative justice might be a more creative response than one that simply measures out the penalty in terms of pounds and points per mile per hour over the limit.

There can be no denying that an ordered system of rewards and penalties 'works' for numerous purposes, and that the financial system by which society is ordered fulfils a vital social function. The real difficulty lies in the application of such a system of thought to those whose criminality arises not from a capacity to calculate consequences in that way but from an inability to function within precisely the system within which most of us make our calculations. Between the driver working out that speeding or illegal parking is 'worth the risk' and, at the other extreme, the disordered personalities who carry out the crimes that claim the major headlines, is a mass of the convicted whose crimes arise from a sheer inability to cope, a failure to make good within the system at all, even, in many cases, from being themselves the victims of the neglect, abuse, greed or persistent violence of others.

For them, that is for those who experience suggests are the vast majority of our prison population, a system that derives its attractiveness from being the kind of system of tariffs and debts with which daily life makes us familiar stands no chance of achieving either of the things that are claimed for it: deterrence or reform. For them the aim has to be a form of restoration, something that places them or places them back (if they have ever been there) within the society from which they are estranged and which, by their actions, they have in turn estranged from themselves.

The estrangement involves the particular victim of their crime, naturally enough, but the best restorative processes go well beyond that so as to recognize that no crime is limited in its effects to the one person or group that has been injured. Criminality witnesses to a mutual disruption of relationships, a social dislocation.

remedies for bankruptcy

It is worth pressing a little further our examination of the effects of the widespread intrusion of an essentially financial mode of thinking on the struggle against the crime figures. For are not those whom we have just described placed in a position analogous to bankruptcy? Bankrupts are judged unable to manage their own affairs (or they would not have become bankrupt), and so they have to be managed; the current designation of the prison and probation services under the heading of 'offender management' is a significant example of the way in which those convicted of crime become less than subjects, units to be managed.

Or, since we are dealing with a whole social caste, perhaps we might better compare their situation with that of debtor countries in a system of world trade that renders their debts fundamentally unrepayable. Recent campaigns about international debt by and large advocated the view that the system of world trade, founded as it is upon calculation, upon systems of monetary settlement in which people and nations are meant to have confidence, can only be said to work adequately if it has some means of 'restoring' the fortunes of those people and nations whose circumstances have rendered it impossible for them to participate – usually because their indebtedness has reached a level where it will be permanently paralysing and bar people from any reasonable standard of life. Faced with that reality, the rest of the trading world has either to find ways of rescuing the situation that allow the system to remain intact or else examine those features of the system that make the participation of the poor impossible – that is, examine their own responsibility for the 'bankruptcy' of the poor, their own complicity in their fate.

That is restoration in a financial setting, and it is not far removed from what restoration would be in the realm of criminality. Processes of restorative justice have to be relational; they cannot function within the cold logic of a system of calculation, tariffs, debts and the rest, because it is precisely that system within which those who engage in criminal behaviour have found themselves defeated. Such processes have to require the taking of responsibility by all those complicit in what has taken place. That may involve the particular victim in receiving the remorse of the perpetrator of the crime. But more than that, it must involve a real engagement by the majority community with those features of its common life whose dislocation has resulted in some individual's or group's manifesting the violence, the greed or the self-centredness that do belong to them, but certainly not to them alone. The social image of restorative justice, as described within many settings, cultures and religious traditions, is that of the circle as both means and goal of restoration: the place of recovered mutuality, of the end of scapegoating, minimizing and alibi, and their replacement by identification, realistic acknowledgement of fault, and a determination to stay in relationship.

the ancient wisdom of restoration

The Hebrew and Christian Scriptures display an intimate knowledge of the financial and economic circumstances of their day.[3] Because those arrangements lack the sophistication and technical development to which we have become accustomed, it is easy to suppose that they also fall behind in wisdom about the fundamental objectives of an economic system. The parable of the labourers in the vineyard in Matthew 20 demonstrates both: the scene presupposes a rural society with no developed 'welfare state' to deal with the problems of unemployment, and a fairly unquestioning system of authority. So some labourers are not hired and, as the day proceeds, there remains a hard core of the unemployed. It is at the point of settlement, however, that there appears a breakthrough, not one that all find comfortable, as the labourers are paid a day's wage irrespective of the hours they have toiled.

At this point people behave very much in character. Those who have toiled long and hard see it as profoundly unfair that their reward is the same as that of the latecomers. The owner defends his action simply on the basis that he is the owner and that it is for him to do as he pleases with his own money. Yet Jesus, in his one-sentence commentary, declares that this behaviour-in-character is also a clue to a much larger policy issue: this essentially commercial transaction, this microcosm of the labour market, has to 'work' not just in terms of fairness or profitability; it has to 'work' also in terms of its capacity to be a place of restoration for those who would otherwise be excluded. This exercise in agricultural production cannot be said to be 'working' if its result is the consigning of four-fifths of the labour force to starvation. So the owner, arbitrary as his generosity is, places the requirements of restoration above the simple requirements of fairness. And, lest anyone should fail to see that this story, while economic, is also social and political in its implications, the event is set in a vineyard, the classic image of God's chosen people, Israel. For the vineyard to be God's it has to be a place of restoration, of something more than fairness, even when being more than fairness strikes some as something less.

This particular parable is all of a piece with a deeply-rooted biblical tradition: it describes a jubilee event, a holy year of restoration, where the circle of humanity is restored. The jubilee traditions are essentially about how something more than fairness – the remission of debts, the restoration of people to their family inheritance – is on offer, precisely because no system, however fair, can produce restoration unless there is deliberate intervention to bring it about. This more-than-fairness is supposed to be a general policy, generally restorative of those for whom fairness will not be sufficient to bring them back to the circle of humanity. So in Matthew 18 the servant who experiences the remission of a large debt and responds by a rigorous enforcement of the system of repayment so that he himself will not find himself in the same helpless position again finds that what his former creditor actually had in mind was a *change of policy* to one in which others too would experience the more-than-fairness that has the potential to restore community.

The wisdom of the parables in particular, and of the biblical tradition in general, lies in the perception that justice can only be secured if the judicial – like the economic – system has enough spaces in it for the restorative process to go on. Nobody can be restored to the human community, nor can the human community itself be restored, if it demands that the structure of calculating fairness be rigidly enforced at all times and for all persons, however marginalized. The jubilee traditions are not in that sense simply altruistic: they recognize that, without spaces for restoration, the system itself will generate an underclass with destructive effects on the whole of society. The 'unjust steward' of Luke 16 demonstrates – albeit in a way that disturbs our moral sensibilities (but the parables are not moral tales but real life stories) – that opportunism and flexibility gain for the about-to-be sacked steward some security, for the debtors some relief, and for the owner of the vineyard some repayment, to an extent that social and economic rigidity, a demand by each for their *due*, would never have achieved.

a restorative rationality

This essay has attempted to suggest both the wisdom of restorative provision and the reasons why that wisdom has a tendency to be rejected. The calls for 'fairness' and for punishments that 'fit the crime' are wholly to be expected when the alternative appears to be 'soft' on the criminal. Yet our system of criminal justice displays all the negative outcomes of a society without jubilee, and it is significant that some of the 'alternatives' to prison seem to arise at the point when the society that demands punishment discovers that it is punishing itself by its reflex resort to imprisonment. The signs are there: the steady rise in the numbers in prison with all the costs that entails in finance and in the quality of prison regimes, in the incidence of self-harm among the imprisoned and sickness and stress among officers. Remedies are being proposed that respond to the presenting difficulties in the system. But what would be most valuable would be the acceptance of a rationality, as well as the implementation of some good practices, that represents a serious commitment to providing spaces of restoration for victims of crime, those convicted of criminal offences and society at large as a key aim of our criminal justice system.

Is it too much to expect that our fellow-citizens and their newspaper writers, representing as they do the entirely understandable responses of those who have 'borne the burden and heat of the day' as they see it, or who find themselves frustrated beyond bearing at the incidence of crime in society, might at some point appreciate the wisdom of seeing our shared need of restoration as offering a better solution to the problem of criminality? The germ of insight is there in the determination to be 'tough on the causes of crime' and to invent more imaginative ways of dealing with those now in prison. What is missing is the determination to present such expedients, and even more imaginative ways of restoring the criminal to the common life of humanity through a serious facing of responsibility, as being themselves images of the restoration that is the common need of human beings, as moral as 'fairness' and at this point in our social history far more creative.

What would indeed be a vision worth pursuing is a pattern of dealing with crime not by the patterns of thought formed in us by the monetary system most of us are fortunate enough to manage to use day by day, but by the patterns of human relationship, of dealing with hurt and guilt, with which we are familiar in the more intimate settings of our lives. Were we to pursue such a vision, to accept the relational rationality that we generally know is the only way forward in the facing of guilt, we would be likely to find that we had pursued not just the kinder but also the wiser course.

notes

introduction – Peter Sedgwick

1. Board for Social Responsibility, *Crime, Justice and the Demands of the Gospel*, GS Misc. 359, 1991.
2. Board for Social Responsibility, *Prisons: a Study in Vulnerability*, Church House Publishing, 1999.
3. From *The New English Bible*, Oxford University Press and Cambridge University Press, 1970.

chapter 1   the reform of sentencing and the future of criminal courts – David Faulkner

1. *Iliad*, xviii.497–508. For a commentary, including references to previous scholarship, see Mark Edwards, *The Iliad: A Commentary* Vol V, Books 17–20, Cambridge University Press, 1991, pp. 213–18. Disappointingly, the poet does not disclose the outcome.
2. John Croft, 'Crime and Morality', *Justice Reflections* 2/12, 2003.
3. Leon Radzinowicz, *Adventures in Criminology*, Routledge, 1999, p. 116.
4. Bhikhu Parekh, 'Common Belonging' in *Cohesion, Community and Citizenship*, Proceedings of a Runnymede Conference, Runnymede Trust, 2002.
5. The term 'liberal' is now the subject of much confusion, with 'neo-liberal' being used to define economic and sometimes social policies based on markets, competition and freedom of choice, together with a minimum of regulation or interference by the state but often accompanied by repressive criminal justice measures to control crime. Such measures are likely to be the antithesis of the liberal tradition described in the text.
6. Philip Bobbitt, *The Shield of Achilles: War, Peace and the Course of History*, Penguin Press, 2002.
7. Peter Hitchens, *A Brief History of Crime*, Atlantic, 2003. Roger Scruton, *The West and the Rest: Globalization and the Terrorist Threat*, ISI Books, 2002.
8. Human rights are usually thought of as those protected by the European Convention on Human Rights and the Human Rights Act 1998. They include the right to life, freedom from torture or degrading punishment, liberty and a fair trial, respect for private and family life, and freedom of thought and expression. Some of those rights are absolute (freedom from torture); most are limited and allow for exceptions, but on the condition, for example, that any interference must be no more than is necessary in a democratic society. Critics argue that the Convention and the Act allow disaffected individuals or organizations to complain of alleged breaches in an attempt to promote their own selfish interests against those of others or of society as a whole. Supporters argue that the significance of formally recognized human rights is that they strengthen society by creating a culture of respect for the rights of others, and a stronger sense of mutual obligations and responsibilities, including those between the citizen and the state. The courts have on the whole taken a fairly restrictive view of the Human Rights Act, and purely selfish or manipulative claims are not likely to succeed.
9. Portia's speech on behalf of Antonio is in *The Merchant of Venice*, Act 4, Scene 1, 179–200. Isabella's plea to Angelo and their subsequent exchange are in *Measure for*

Measure, Act 1, Scene 2, 99–123. Both Portia and Isabella attack the idea that the process of justice must always take its course, regardless of its effect on individuals. Angelo responds to Isabella by claiming, in effect – as some might do today – that pity for future victims, and perhaps even regard for public opinion, takes precedence over any regard for the individual offender. Isabella replies that it is 'good to have a giant's strength, but tyrannous to use it like a giant'; and expresses her contempt for 'man, proud man, Dressed in a little brief authority . . .'

10. Timothy Gorringe, *God's Just Vengeance*, Cambridge University Press, 1996, pp. 223–71.

11. David McIlroy, 'The Holy Spirit and the Law', *Justice Reflections* 3.14, 2003.

12. Christopher Marshall, 'Prison, Prisoners and the Bible', *Justice Reflections* 3.13, 2003. Stuart Dew, 'Why Should Christians be Concerned about Criminal Justice?', *Justice Reflections*, 2/11, 2003.

13. Jonathan Burnside, 'Inspired Justice', lecture given to the Lawyers' Christian Fellowship, 7 September 2001 and published in *Justice Reflections*, 1/1, 2002.

14. From a chapter by Jonathan Burnside in a forthcoming book from the Jubilee Centre (title and publication date to be announced).

15. Nicola Lacey, 'Principles, Politics and Criminal Justice' in Lucia Zedner and Andrew Ashworth (eds), *The Criminological Foundations of Penal Policy*, Clarendon Press, 2003. David Downes and Rod Morgan, 'The Skeletons in the Cupboard: the Politics of Law and Order at the Turn of the Millennium' in Mike Maguire, Rod Morgan and Robert Reiner (eds), *The Oxford Handbook of Criminology*, third edition, Oxford University Press, 2002, pp. 286–321.

16. Labour governments in office have not generally been noted for a liberal approach to crime or criminal justice. Home Secretaries who are remembered as 'liberal' reformers have usually been members of Conservative governments – Peel, Butler, Hurd – or of Liberal governments – Churchill or his less well-known predecessor Herbert Gladstone. Gladstone, together with officials such as Evelyn Ruggles-Brise, the Chairman of the Prison Commission, was responsible for the reforms of 1906–1910 relating to the treatment of children and the introduction of probation and borstal training (he had previously been chairman of the committee that produced the Gladstone Report on prisons). Even Roy Jenkins owed his liberal reputation more to social reforms in matters such as racial and sexual equality than to his penal policies.

17. Board for Social Responsibility, *Crime, Justice and the Demands of the Gospel*, General Synod Board for Social Responsibility, 1991.

18. Peter Neyroud and Alan Beckley are among several authors who have considered the damage centrally imposed targets and performance indicators can cause to the integrity of policing (Neyroud and Beckley, *Policing, Ethics and Human Rights*, Willan Publishing, 2001).

19. Home Office, *Justice for All*, Cm 5563, Stationery Office, 2002.

20. The information is contained in Home Office Digest 4 – *Information on the Criminal Justice System*, p. 29, periodically up-dated and available at http://www.homeoffice.gov.uk/rds/digest4/chapter4pdf, p. 4. The percentage relates to the volume of crime that is uncovered by the British Crime Survey, from which certain offences are excluded because they are very rare (for example murder and rape), or because there is no direct or identifiable victim.

21. The Conservative government during the 1980s was to some extent an exception. Crime prevention and support for victims both became important aspects of government policy. Both were promoted by, and to a large extent relied upon, voluntary organizations such as NACRO (as it then was), Crime Concern and Victim Support, working in partnership with, but outside, the formal criminal justice system.

22. 'Net-widening' or 'thinning the mesh' is a subject about which criminologists have expressed concern for many years. Their concern is that the more people, and especially young people and children, become the subject of criminal proceedings, the more likely they are to become stigmatized and behave as criminals (see Stan Cohen, *Visions of Social Control: Crime, Punishment and Classification*, Polity Press, 1985).

23. David Blunkett, 'How Government can help build Social Capital', speech to a Performance and Innovation Unit seminar on 26 March 2002, Home Office, London.

24. Risk assessment has become a major activity in criminal justice. The techniques are based on the statistical likelihood that a person will reoffend, taking account of his or her background, circumstances and previous criminal record. Their use is mainly to devise a programme for their treatment in prison or while under supervision that will make their reoffending less likely, but an assessment of risk might also affect decisions on bail or discretionary release, or the actual sentence of the court. Decisions that, in effect, increase the severity of a person's punishment for reasons unrelated to their offence or current behaviour would raise questions of natural justice and possibly human rights.

25. Archbishop Rowan Williams, *The Richard Dimbleby Lecture 2002*, Church of England, 2002, available on the Archbishop of Canterbury's web site: www.archbishopofcanterbury.org.uk/sermons_speeches/021219.html

26. There has been a trend in criminal justice legislation towards giving courts, or sometimes the police or other authorities, a power to issue an order to a person to do or refrain from doing something, disobedience to which then becomes a criminal offence often punishable by a severe sentence of imprisonment. The antisocial behaviour order introduced under the Crime and Disorder Act 1998 is the most obvious example, but others are to be found in the Criminal Justice and Public Order Act 1994, the Prevention of Harassment Act 1997, the Anti-Social Behaviour Act 2003, and in proposals contained in the Domestic Violence, Crime and Victims Bill announced in the Queen's Speech on 26 November 2003. The behaviour that gives rise to the order need not itself be criminal. The purpose is to provide an effective sanction against behaviour that falls short of a criminal offence or where a prosecution may be difficult. Critics are concerned that, as well as 'widening the net', the eventual sanction of imprisonment might be wholly out of proportion to the behaviour concerned.

27. See Lord Justice Auld, *Report of a Review of the Criminal Courts of England and Wales* (the Auld Report), Stationery Office, 2001; John Halliday, *Making Punishments Work: Report of a Review of the Sentencing Framework for England and Wales* (the Halliday Report), Home Office, 2001; Home Office, *Justice for All*, 2003, and *Respect and Responsibility: Taking a Stand Against Anti-Social Behaviour*, Cm 5778, Stationery Office, 2003.

28. Deterrence is clearly a part of the instrumental aim of sentencing, although the Court of Appeal in its judgment in *Cunningham* in 1992 seemed to regard it as indistinguishable from retribution. There is little or no evidence that increased severity in sentencing has any deterrent effect (see Andrew Von Hirsch, Andrew Ashworth, Elizabeth Burney and P. O. Wilkstrom, *Criminal Deterrence and Sentence Severity*, Hart Publishing, 1999).

29. Anthony Duff, *Punishment, Communication and Community*, Oxford University Press, 2001. See also 'Restoration and Retribution' in Andrew Von Hirsch, Julian Roberts, Anthony Bottoms, Kent Roach, and Mara Schiff (eds), *Restorative Justice and Criminal Justice: Competing or Reconcilable Paradigms?* Hart Publishing, 2002, pp. 43–60.
30. Home Office, *Justice for All*, 2003.
31. Michael Hough, Jessica Jacobson and Andrew Millie, *The Decision to Imprison: Sentencing and the Prison Population*, Prison Reform Trust, 2003.
32. Patrick Carter, *Managing Offenders, Reducing Crime*, Prime Minister's Strategy Unit, 2004.
33. Home Office, *Reducing Crime – Changing Lives*, Home Office, 2004.
34. Archbishop Rowan Williams, The Children's Society National Festival Service, Canterbury Cathedral 2003, available on the Archbishop of Canterbury's web site (as note 25 above, /030920 html).
35. Department for Education and Skills, *Every Child Matters*, Department for Education and Skills, 2003.
36. Home Office, *Youth Justice – the Next Steps*, Home Office, 2003.
37. Audit Commission, *Youth Justice 2004*, Audit Commission, 2004.
38. Comptroller and Auditor General, *Youth Offending: The Delivery of Community and Custodial Sentences*, HC 190 Session 2003–2004, Stationery Office, 2004.
39. Audit Commission, *Youth Justice 2004*.
40. Ros Burnett and Catherine Appleton, *Joined-up Youth Justice: Tackling Youth Crime in Partnership*, Russell House Publishing, forthcoming.
41. See for example the report *Children in Trouble*, by Geoff Monaghan, Pam Hibbert and Sharon Moore (2003), published by Barnardo's and promoted jointly by Barnardo's, The Children's Rights Alliance for England, The Children's Society, The Howard League for Penal Reform, Nacro, The National Association for Youth Justice, The National Children's Bureau, NCH and NSPCC. For an analysis of the implications of the Green Paper *Youth Justice – the Next Steps* and its relationship with the Green Paper *Every Child Matters*, see Nacro's *Youth Crime Briefing* for December 2003.
42. Home Office, *Justice for All*, 2003.
43. Home Office, *Youth Justice – the Next Steps*, 2003.
44. David Blunkett, *Civil Renewal: A New Agenda*, Home Office, 2003.
45. Hazel Blears, 'Communities in control: public services and local socialism', Fabian Society, 2003.
46. Office for National Statistics, 'Investing in Each Other and the Community: the Role of Social Capital', *Social Trends*, 33rd edition, 2003, pp. 19–27.
47. David Faulkner, *Crime, State and Citizen: A Field Full of Folk*, Waterside Press, 2001. David Faulkner, 'Taking Citizenship Seriously: Social Capital and Citizenship in a Changing World', *Criminal Justice* 3/3, 2003, pp. 287–315.
48. David Blunkett, *Civil Renewal*, 2003.
49. Tim Newburn, 'Atlantic Crossings: Policy Transfer and Crime Control in England and Wales', *Punishment and Society* 4/12, 2002, pp. 165–94.
50. The United States Attorneys' Bulletin, published by the Department of Justice in Washington DC, devoted a special issue (49/1, January 2001) to 'Community Prosecution'. An article by John Feinblatt and Greg Berman from the Center for Court Innovation described the Red Hook Community Justice Center as follows:

Red Hook is the nation's first multi-jurisdictional community court. Operating out of a refurbished Catholic school, the Justice Center seeks to solve neighbourhood problems like drugs, crime, domestic violence and landlord-tenant disputes. At Red Hook, a single judge hears neighbourhood cases that under ordinary circumstances would go to three different courts – Civil, Family and Criminal. The goal is to offer a coordinated, rather than piecemeal, approach to the problems of families and communities. The Red Hook judge has an array of sanctions and services at his disposal, including community restitution projects, on-site job training, drug treatment and mental health counselling – all rigorously monitored to ensure accountability and drive home notions of individual responsibility.

The Red Hook story goes far beyond what happens in the courtroom. The courthouse is the hub for an array of unconventional programs that engage local residents in 'doing justice'. These include mediation, community service projects that put local volunteers to work repairing conditions of disorder and a 'youth court' where teenagers resolve actual cases involving their peers. The concept is to engage communities in aggressive crime prevention. This strategy works in two ways – it solves local problems before they even come to court and it helps knit together the fabric of the neighbourhood.

The article goes on to consider some of the 'hot-button' issues that arise – 'net widening', judicial values, and the appearance of being 'soft on crime'. Other articles consider wider questions of the role of public prosecutors and public defenders in their local communities and in relation to local communities and the issues of principle that arise from it. It is difficult to see how the model of Red Hook, especially its combination of jurisdictions under a single judge, could be translated directly to a court in England and Wales without new legislation. But the pilot project the Home Office has established in Liverpool (Home Office Press Release CJS 007/2003, 11 September) is an interesting venture, which deserves support.

chapter 2   restorative justice in England – Tim Newell

1. Albert Eglash, 'Beyond Restitution: Creative Restitution' in Joe Hudson and Burt Galaway (eds), *Restitution in Criminal Justice*, D. C. Heath, 1977.
2. Jeschke Marlin, 'A Christian Approach to Criminal Justice', *Brethren Life and Thought. A Quarterly Journal*, Vol. XXIX, Winter, Number One, 1984.
3. René Girard, *The Scapegoat* (trans. Yvonne Freccero), Athlone, 1986.
4. Pierre Allard and Wayne Northey, 'Christianity: the Rediscovery of Restorative Justice' in Michael Hadley (ed.), *The Spiritual Roots of Restorative Justice*, State University of New York Press, 2001.
5. Ruth Morris, *A Practical Path to Transformative Justice*, Rittenhouse, 1994.
6. This definition was promoted at the Restorative Justice Consortium conference in November 2002.
7. Helen Reeves, 'The Victim Support Perspective' in M. Wright and B. Galaway (eds), *Victims, Offenders and Community*, Sage Publications, 1989.
8. John Braithwaite, *Crime, Shame and Reintegration*, Cambridge University Press, 1989.

9. *Restorative Justice: The Government's Strategy*, HMSO, July 2003.

10. Desmond Tutu, *No Future Without Forgiveness*, Rider Books, 1999.

11. Morris, *A Practical Path to Transformative Justice*, 1994.

12. Conrad Brunk, 'Restorative Justice and the Philosophical Theories of Criminal Punishment' in Michael Hadley (ed.), *The Spiritual Roots of Restorative Justice*, State University of New York Press, 2001.

13. Richard Holloway, *On Forgiveness: How Can We Forgive the Unforgivable?*, Canongate, 2002.

14. Henri Nouwen, *The Return of the Prodigal Son*, Image Books, 1994, pp. 98–9.

15. A report of the interdisciplinary Spiritual Roots Project is in Michael Hadley's *The Justice Tree: multifaith reflection on criminal justice*, Center for Studies in Religion and Society, Victoria, 2002.

16. Joseph Campbell, *The Power of Myth*, Viking Penguin Inc., 1972.

17. William Blake, in Arthur Lee and Daniel Nicholson (eds), *The Oxford Book of English Mystical Verse*, Oxford University Press, 1917.

Further note: In addition to the works cited in the notes above, the author wishes to recommend the following as further reading on this subject:

Nils Christie, *Limits to Pain,* Universitersforleger, 1981.

Michael Hadley, *The Spiritual Roots of Restorative Justice*, State University of New York Press, 2001.

John Lampen, *Mending Hurts*, Quaker Home Service, 1987.

Tony F. Marshall and Susan Merry, *Crime and Accountability: Victim/Offender Mediation in Practice*, Home Office, HMSO, 1990.

Paul McCold, 'Restorative Justice and the Role of Community' in Burt Falaway and Joe Hudson (eds), *Restorative Justice: International Perspectives*, Criminal Justice Press, 1996.

D. L. Nathanson, *Shame and Pride: Affects, Sex and the Birth of the Self*, W. W. Norton, 1992.

Sylvan Tomkins, 'Affect/Imagery/Consciousness' in J. Aronoff, A.I. Rabin and R. A. Zucker (eds), *The Emergence of Personality*, Springer, 1962.

Mark Umbreit, *Victim Meets Offender: The Impact of Restorative Justice and Mediation*, Willow Tree Press, Inc., 1990.

Jim Wallis, *The Soul of Politics: Beyond 'Religious Right' and 'Secular Left'*, Harcourt Brace & Company, 1995.

Martin Wright, *Justice for Victims and Offenders: A Restorative Response to Crime*, Open University Press, 1991.

Howard Zehr, *Changing Lenses: A New Focus for Crime and Justice*, Herald Press, 1990.

chapter 3   responsible sentencing – Stephen Pryor

1. HMSO, February 1991.

2. Geese Theatre Company is the only national touring company in the UK to work primarily within the Criminal Justice System. The main focus of its work is to challenge offending behaviour through drama and theatre with offenders either in prison or on probation. For more information see www.geese.co.uk

3. This report was published in November 2001 and can be found on the following web sites: www.hmprisonservice.gov.uk; www.homeoffice.gov.uk
4. See www.rethinking.org.uk
5. This can be found at www.ccjf.org/what/index.html
6. OASys is the new National Offender IT Assessment System, developed jointly by the Prison and Probation Services.
7. This is a partnership whereby prisoners from Springhill open prison have been trained, and work, as Citizens Advisers in the Oxford Citizens Advice Bureau.

chapter 4   the churches and criminal justice – Stuart Dew

1. Paraphrased from Jane Clay, 'Prisoners and their Beliefs' in Christopher Jones and Peter Sedgwick (eds), *The Future of Criminal Justice*, SPCK, 1995.
2. William Noblett, *Prayers for People in Prison*, Oxford University Press, 1998.
3. William Noblett, *Prayers for People in Prison*, 1998.
4. John King (ed.), *The Probation and After Care Service* (Third Edition), Butterworths, 1969.
5. Thomas Holmes, *Pictures and Problems of the London Police Courts*, Thomas Nelson and Sons, 1900, quoted in Joan F. S. King, 'ILPAS '76, a report to commemorate the centenary of probation in London', ILPAS, 1976.
6. Alpha for Prisons: www.caringforexoffenders.org
7. The Mothers' Union: www.themothersunion.org
8. Pacer 50plus: www.olderprisoners.co.uk
9. Care Remand Fostering: www.remandfostering.org.uk
10. Depaul Trust: www.depaultrust.org
11. The Prison Advice and Care Trust: www.imprisonment.org.uk
12. Prison Fellowship: www.prisonfellowship.org.uk
13. Surrey Appropriate Adult Volunteer Scheme: www.saavs.org.
14. Revive Enterprise: email paul@smartp19.freeserve.co.uk
15. Amelia Methodist Trust: tel: 01446 781427; www.barrywales.co.uk/ameliatrust
16. Oxford Youth Works: tel: 01865 204646.
17. Kainos Community: www.kainoscommunity.org
18. Stepping Stones: www.steppingstonestrust.org.uk
19. National Association of Official Prison Visitors: www.naopv.org.uk
20. Prisoners' Penfriends: email gwyn.morgan@prisonerspenfriends.org
21. Inside Out Trust: www.inside-out.org.uk
22. Parents in Prison, PO Box 55, Royston, Hertfordshire, SG8 5GE.
23. National Association of Victims Support Schemes: www.victimsupport.org
24. For information about lay magistrates: www.magistrates-association.org.uk
25. Board for Social Responsibility, *Meeting the Challenge, How Churches Should Respond to Sex Offenders*, 1999.
26. *Women in Prison*, Catholic Agency for Social Concern, 1999.
27. Social Exclusion Unit, *Reducing Re-offending by Ex-prisoners*, Social Exclusion Unit, 2002.
28. See note 27.

29. Prison Advice and Care Trust on behalf of Churches' Criminal Justice Forum, funded by Rethinking Crime and Punishment, *What Can I Do? How you can get involved in the criminal justice system*, 2002. Available from CCJF, 39 Eccleston Square, London, SW1V 1BX or email dews@cbcew.org.uk
30. The CCJF web site is at www.ccjf.org.uk

chapter 6   restorative justice in a money culture – Peter Selby

1. Conrad G. Brunk, 'Restorative Justice and the Philosophical Theories of Criminal Punishment' in Michael L. Hadley (ed.), *The Spiritual Roots of Restorative Justice*, State University of New York, 2001, pp. 54f.
2. From a speech given by the Rt Hon. David Blunkett MP, Home Secretary, to the Police Federation in May 2003.
3. See Peter Selby, *Grace and Mortgage: the Language of Faith and the Debt of the World*, Darton, Longman & Todd, 1997.

general index

index of biblical references